The Bourgeois Interior

Bourgeois Interior

JULIA
PREWITT
BROWN

University of Virginia Press
CHARLOTTESVILLE AND LONDON

University of Virginia Press
© 2008 by the Rector and Visitors of the University of Virginia
All rights reserved
Printed in the United States of America on acid-free paper

First published 2008

9 8 7 6 5 4 3 2 1

LIBRARY OF CONGRESS CATALOGING-IN-PUBLICATION DATA

Brown, Julia Prewitt, 1948–
    The bourgeois interior / Julia Prewitt Brown.
        p.   cm.
    Includes bibliographical references and index.
    ISBN 978-0-8139-2710-7 (acid-free paper)
    1. English fiction—History and criticism. 2. Middle class in literature.
3. Interior decoration in literature. 4. Dwellings in literature. 5. Middle
class in art. 6. Interior decoration in art. 7. Dwellings in art. 8. American
fiction—History and criticism. I. Title.
    PR830.M53B76   2008
    820.9′355—dc22   2008003089

For Howard Eiland

Contents

Illustrations

Preface

No one likes to think of himself as bourgeois. Yet the signs of bourgeois society are all around us. We have only to examine the array of "home magazines" on display in any drugstore, from bargain basement, do-it-yourself decorating magazines to catalogs of "luxury estates," to be reminded of the ubiquity of bourgeois values. *Embourgeoisement,* or the process by which all classes come to identify with the interests and aspirations of the middle class, is apparent throughout our society, from a "laboring class" with substantial pension funds invested in Wall Street to an "upper class" with socioeconomic aspirations very similar to those of the middle class. (Consider the wedding pages of the *New York Times.*) In the conclusion to this work, I refer to the present or technological age as an "afterlife" of the nineteenth-century bourgeoisie, or one in which old-bourgeois myths are still pervasive.

A few decades ago Roland Barthes defined the bourgeoisie as "the social class which does not want to be named." This flight from the word *bourgeois,* he insisted, is not accidental: "it is bourgeois ideology itself," the process by which bourgeois norms are experienced as "the evident laws of natural order."[1] Yet to the bourgeois, immersion in a false nature is by no means as reassuring as the well-known imputation of bourgeois "complacency" makes it sound. A subtle example of this is implied at the opening of Witold Rybczynski's witty contribution to bourgeois history, *Home: A Short History of an Idea.* "During the six years of my architectural education," the author observes, "the subject of comfort was mentioned only once."[2] Comfort is a bourgeois value par excellence, which is not to say that "comfort" is always comforting. One has only to buy a mattress to make this discovery. In the sales literature for mattresses, the words *pain* and *sleeplessness* appear almost as frequently as the word *comfort,* as if everyone who bought a mattress is seeking relief from insomnia and muscular pain. In bourgeois society, the pursuit of comfort is itself a sign of agitation and unrest.

This book does not aim to unmask the bourgeois. It aims to focus attention on the mask itself, or on the protective material expressions of bourgeois life. Neither is it a materialist study of bourgeois "things." Catalogs of objects figure in histories of bourgeois culture like Asa Briggs's *Victorian Things,* but they are of interest here only in so far as the bourgeois himself loves to catalog his things. To the bourgeois, objects are alive, which is something he has in common with the child. No work illustrates this point more movingly than Walter Benjamin's *Berlin Childhood around 1900.*

To grasp the elusive concept of "bourgeois" in the contemporary context, I made myself into a kind of suburban flâneur. The American suburbs are far from possessing the phantasmagoric variety of the famed nineteenth-century flâneur's stomping ground, Paris, but they have plenty to occupy the attention of anyone interested in understanding what it means to be bourgeois. In combing real estate ads, attending open houses, and taking long walks where sidewalks were available, I was often reminded of the Latin root of the word *bourgeois,* which is *burgus,* meaning *fortress.* Elaborate security systems, "invisible fences," and "granite kitchens" are prime selling features of suburban real estate. Yet like that of the mattresses with their discomfiting literature about steel metal coils, the ostensible goal of these dwellings is comfort. Only after this initial stage of exploration was I able to approach the literary subject of the book, a fact that I bore in mind when I added contemporary references. I am convinced that whatever is both amusing and profound, both charming and disturbing, about the bourgeois domestic interior in literature is more readily grasped by a reader who is alive to the present in the past, the past in the present.

In discussing selected works of literary and visual art, I more often use the words *bourgeois imagination of life* than *bourgeois ideology* for a reason. It's not simply that the richness of these works, their intrinsic variety and texture, is greater than the promulgation of ideology allows for. (Compare, for example, the endlessly renewed complexity of Vermeer's *The Love Letter,* reproduced on page 7, with the strident ideographs of country cottages by Thomas Kinkade on sale in shopping malls throughout America.) It's that I share the skepticism of historians like J. G. A. Pocock in recognizing that "bourgeois ideology" is itself a problematic concept. In his analysis of the tension between "virtue and commerce" in the eighteenth century, Pocock insists that "there is no greater and no commoner mistake in the history of social thought than to suppose that the tension ever disappeared, and that the ideals of virtue and unity of personality were driven from the field, or that a commercial, 'liberal' or 'bourgeois' ideology reigned undisturbed until challenged by the harbingers of Marx." According to Pocock, there has always been an "ambivalent dialogue" over the emergence of bourgeois norms.[3] I have tried to be attentive to this ambivalence throughout my discussion.

I would like to acknowledge the following people and institutions for their generous support of this project. Cathie Brettschneider, Humanities Editor at the University of Virginia Press, has been a joy to work with. The two anonymous readers at the press gave tactful and discerning recommendations for revision. David Thorburn and James Winn were extremely generous with their time, encouragement, and wise insight. Bonnie Costello, Marcia Folsom, Carol McGuirk, Susan Mizruchi, Lee Monk, Barbara Schapiro, Steven Tapscott, Sandra Tropp, and Elizabeth Yates read parts of an earlier draft and gave invaluable suggestions. For inspiring conversation about the questions raised in the book, I would like to thank Elizabeth Brown, Ruah Donnelly, Susan Jackson, Margery Kirber, Leshan Kwan, Naomi Miller, and Swen Voekel. For the illustrations I am grateful to the Rijksmuseum, Amsterdam; the Swedish Film Institute, Svensk Filmindustri; and the Museum of Fine Arts, Boston.

My greatest debt is to my husband, Howard Eiland. As Mr. Pickwick says to Mr. Perker: "You have done me many acts of kindness that I can never repay, and have no wish to repay, for I prefer continuing the obligation."

The Bourgeois Interior

Introduction

Look around this room of yours, and what do you see? John Ruskin posed this question to bourgeois readers in 1853. How would middle-class readers answer it today?

Standing at the outside of a typical bourgeois residence in suburban Boston in 2006, we are likely to see evidence of a security system, perhaps in the form of a small red light near the entrance, and a plaque identifying the company that designed the system. A peephole in the door makes it possible for the dweller to view the outside world through a distorting lens. As in Robinson Crusoe's island fortress—the first bourgeois interior in English fiction—a surveillance and warning system protects against unlawful entry. The name of a security service in the metropolitan area would have appealed to Robinson Crusoe: "Absolute Security, Inc."

Entering the living room, we may notice objects collected from abroad, not unlike the souvenirs and art objects displayed in the Meagleses' interior in Dickens's *Little Dorrit* (1855–57) or at Waterbath in James's *The Spoils of Poynton* (1897). Though designed in different styles, the contemporary living room and family room replicate the drawing and sitting rooms of the nineteenth-century bourgeois household, separate spheres—psychologically and socially—in both periods. The architect Sarah Susanka points out that the formal living room is rarely used in the American home. Accordingly, we may notice a certain unlived-in look in the living room and the suggestion in its arrangement of furniture that things are on display. As in Jane Austen's grand bourgeois residences, the bourgeois interior is meant to be shown.

Like their encased Victorian counterparts, objects in today's interiors are to be found in containers. There is a container for something in every room: in the foyer, a stand to hold umbrellas; in the bathroom, a container in which to put a cardboard box of tissues; in the family room, an armoire to enclose a television. "What didn't the nineteenth century invent some casing for!" exclaimed Walter Benjamin,[1] prophesying the creation of immensely profitable companies like "The Container Store" and "Holds Everything, Inc." In the living room, one also notices objects from nature presented in some ideal, petrified state: for example, ceramic fruit in a bowl or artificial flowers in a vase. Nature condemned to eternal life is a sentence delivered in several bourgeois interiors discussed in this book—notably those of Dickens and James. In the family room, other forms of preservation appear: family photographs and relics, such as a bronzed baby shoe. In the bathroom, a monogrammed towel hangs on a bar. The bourgeoisie like to leave traces of themselves, even in the most private spaces.[2]

Many of these features, as we shall see, may be found in domestic interiors of the past. What do they tell us about the people who dwell in them, about their relation to material objects, their experience of themselves and the world? And how has it happened, given radical changes in domestic life over the past three hundred years, that certain features persist? To give an example: we no longer inhabit the domestic interior as we did before the telephone and television became part of middle-class life. "The telephone brings the outside in," writes J. Hillis Miller, "breaks down the inside/outside dichotomy, and endangers the possibility of private communication."[3] Yet the history of our accommodation of the telephone within the home is by no means static.

Some readers may recall in the homes of their grandparents an architectural feature that has since vanished: the telephone room. A small, intimate space intended to keep conversations that went beyond the home private, this feature disappeared with the more open designs of modern building, and it would be unthinkable in a world in which people feel at ease talking on cell phones in public places. The telephone has come and gone as a fixture of the domestic interior, which manages to absorb all sorts of technologies and changes in social organization as if its very purpose were to mediate such forces.

My central thesis is that the bourgeois interior functions as a *medium* through which something is transmitted, a many-layered fabric across which different energies travel: psychological, political, economic, aesthetic, cultural, historical. To say that something is a medium is not the same as saying that it is significant or symbolic. The objects in the interior are not symbols; they are the material out of which symbols are made. They are the plastic and material language—furniture, draperies, wallpaper, bibelots, the symmetrical or asymmetrical arrangement of objects and their (Victorian) plenitude or (modern) spareness, the use of light and shadow, the articulation of space as it refers, or avoids referring, to an "outside"—through which the bourgeoisie expresses itself. Just as an artist works in a medium, one that offers possibilities as well as imposes limitations, so may a social class and the individuals in it.

The domestic interior is a medium in another sense as well, for it conveys messages, which is why artists attend to it, and why people like to sit in the room of a beloved person who has died and gaze upon the objects the beloved touched. "Ah! There's something here that will never be in the inventory!" says Fleda Vetch in *The Spoils of Poynton.* Opening her senses to the interior of a deceased woman who, like herself, has been disappointed in love, Fleda continues: "It's a kind of fourth dimension. It's a presence, a perfume, a touch. It's a soul, a story, a life."[4] In W. G. Sebald's *The Emigrants,* Henry Selwyn also contemplates an inventory with which he is identified when he surveys the automobiles he collected in an earlier life of pleasure and adventure: "The cars are all still in the garage, and they may be worth something now. But I have never been able to bring myself to sell anything, except perhaps, at one point, my soul."[5] In all the works discussed in this book, the inventory of "things" is essential to the bourgeois, but where does the bourgeois stand in relation to it? Does he possess the inventory, Sebald asks, or does the inventory possess him? In the representation of domestic space in fiction, in which *character* and *things* are so closely identified, the bourgeois soul is at once defined and imperiled.

The following pages detail a large mythology, one that might also be explored in histories of popular and material culture. Since the 1950s, television situation comedy has presented us with innumerable portraits of domestic space, and the history of interior decoration is another rich source of information. But it is in literature and art that the heart of this mythology may be found. When we turn to the great painters, novelists, and filmmakers of middle-class domestic life, we turn to those who actually invented or helped to invent the way we see the way we live—or want to live. In studying interiors envisioned by a range of artists over time—Daniel Defoe, Jane Austen, Charles Dickens, Henry James, Virginia Woolf, Ingmar Bergman, John Updike, and W. G. Sebald—we may trace an evolution of bourgeois domestic space together with its sometimes deceptively modest interrogation of what it means to live concretely in the world.

The Bourgeois Class

What do we mean by the word *bourgeois?* On the simplest level, it refers to the class between the very wealthy and the working class. But this definition is misleading for several reasons. As novelists have frequently shown, the very wealthy are also often bourgeois in their view of life, unless they are nobility, in which case they might not be very wealthy at all. The difficulty lies in the fact that the bourgeois or "middle" class is a residual category, comprising those groups that *don't* belong to (a) the working class, or those who perform some kind of manual labor, and (b) a patrician class, even if that class is getting poorer. In nineteenth-century novels, the borders of the bourgeoisie are porous, as we can see when characters travel either down or up into the middle class. The theory of *embourgeoisement* tends to underpin the social vision of novels that treat the subject of social mobility.

Historians like R. S. Neale have shown that the middle classes—and the plural is important—are quite varied if we look at them from the point of view of occupations and incomes. And if we consider different national histories of the bourgeois class, we see even more economic and historical disparities at work. It is in the literature and art of these varied middle-class and national perspectives that a consistent imagination of life emerges that may be called *bourgeois.* Central to this imagination of life is the domestic interior as a medium for the myriad of forces I have just mentioned.

In treating the bourgeoisie as an international social entity, I am relying on the traditional idea of class normally attributed to Marx, which he himself claimed to have derived from the bourgeois historians who preceded him, that sees the existence of the bourgeoisie as bound up with particular phases in the development of production in postfeudal Western countries. Although debate concerning the historical moment of the emergence of a bourgeois class is ongoing—the word *bourgeois* first appeared in French in the early eleventh century—I will be using the word here to refer to the class that emerged in seventeenth-century Holland, in what historians identify as the first bourgeois state.[6] The feudal household had combined living and work, but in the Dutch "Golden Age" of the bourgeoisie, the private family home came into being as something set apart from the public sphere. In the articulation of bourgeois private space in Dutch genre painting, we see bourgeois individuals enjoying their many pleasures, the most fragile of which is that condition of insular stability the bourgeois class would eventually lose. The constant encroachment of the outside world on the middle-class home in Dickens's novels is an especially powerful evocation of this loss. In my final chapter, which considers the "afterlife" of the bourgeoisie, my story of the rise and fall of the middle-class home as a model of life comes to an end with a discussion of stories by Updike and Sebald. If the bourgeoisie has lost much of its social significance in postindustrial society (where the ruling class is no longer the property-owning bourgeoisie, controlling the means of production, but the technocrats and bureaucrats who direct the process of technological innovation and economic growth), these stories show that the mythology of bourgeois domesticity is with us still.

A Comparison

One of the most powerful components of this mythology is the imagination—and memory—of security. If we compare Vermeer's well-known painting *The Love Letter* (ca. 1669–70) with an image created much later in history, long after the effects of industrial capitalism had established themselves, the loss of bourgeois security is nicely epitomized (see pages 7 and 9). A deep interiority pervades *The Love Letter*. Although light is coming into the room from the left, we do not see the window. Vermeer uses a foreground curtain as a *repoussoir*— a compositional device commonly used by Dutch painters to distance a scene—and objects in the foreground, such as the shoes, the broom, and papers, momentarily distract us. But nothing can slow the powerful direction of our gaze as we are rapidly drawn into the image by the diagonals of the checkered floor. The scene itself suggests an intimacy as rich as it is ambiguous. Is the letter being sent or delivered? We feel part of yet distanced from the scene. Our simultaneous absorption in and detachment from its peaceful containment provides a fragile emotional equilibrium. The maidservant has suspended her labor—a broom and laundry basket line the path into the room—to tend to her mistress. Her gaze and posture might be interpreted as both friendly and ironic, her arm resting confidently on her hip as she looks down at the seated figure. The dizzying context for the recessed scene—a rich array of geometric, floral, and decorative patterns—does not seem to impinge

The Love Letter, Jan Vermeer, ca. 1669–70. (Courtesy of the Rijksmuseum, Amsterdam)

on the stable balance of power between mistress and maidservant. Like all of Vermeer's interiors, "a certain hermetic, obsessive, even bewitched element" strikes us in its rendering of ordinary reality, enhancing the sense of enclosure.[7]

Other Dutch genre paintings, though not as mysterious or incandescent as those of Vermeer, also communicate a sense of security. Although over the course of the seventeenth century, artists drew increasingly sharp distinctions between the domains of private and public life, many Dutch paintings suggest a friendly rapport between the world within the home and that which is shown outside of a window or door: warm light invades the room, street musicians offer pleasure, or beggars hover, posing no threat.[8] This harmony of inner and outer contrasts markedly with the way in which the street encroaches on and threatens the security of the home in George Cruikshank's illustrations of nineteenth-century London.

The ideal of the home is ancient, but a specifically bourgeois domestic ideal may be traced to seventeenth-century Holland and to Dutch genre painting. According to recent historians of the home in society and art, the modern vision of the home as "a safeguard to the family's cohesion [and] as the place where we may be our 'true' selves" emerges in these paintings.[9] Many aspects of home life treasured by Dickens, for example, such as the figure of the woman as keeper of the keys, or the comforting presence of architectural spaces for withdrawal within the home, may be traced back to these images. I draw attention to the Dutch ideal because, as we shall see, a sense of loss haunts later visions of the home, and it is important to bear in mind that this nostalgia is not based solely on myth but on a particular historical situation and the art that emerged from it; they seem to have fed one another.

Recent research has shown, for example, that features of the aesthetically pleasing or "ideal" image of the home found in Dutch painting came to be imitated in houses of the period. The perfectly aligned doorways in Emanuel de Witte's classic image of the Dutch home in *Interior with Woman at a Clavichord* (ca. 1660), an alignment that offers a progression of views, was not found in homes of the period until a few decades after the painting appeared.[10] How do we interpret this conversation between art and life? On the one hand, we could say that even in seventeenth-century Holland, where something like a bourgeois paradise existed, there was always a gap between the dream of an interior and the rooms people actually inhabited. On the other hand, the exchange between an idealizing art and social reality seems to have been particularly vital in this pe-

Isak Borg observing the family celebration in a publicity still from *Wild Strawberries,* 1958. (Courtesy of the Svensk Filmindustri and the Swedish Film Institute)

riod in Dutch history. The paintings conveyed a new social reality, and the new social reality drew on art. Life imitates art, as Oscar Wilde remarked, and the role that longing plays in this mimetic impulse is not simple. Nostalgia, at any rate, is something more than what one critic calls a "social disease."[11] It is a function of our love of the past or of our capacity to retain the ideals of earlier generations.

In Ingmar Bergman's *Wild Strawberries* (1958), from which the second image is taken, love and loss of the past are indistinguishable from one another, yet the film is not sentimental. The framing device interrogates the bourgeois interior in a far more unnerving manner than does the use of the *repoussoir* in Vermeer's painting because of the way it positions the main character as lonely outsider. Seventy-eight-year-old Isak Borg stands at the edge of the doorway, the unseen spectator of his own life. In stills unavailable for reproduction, his body forms part of a dark panel that compresses the bright image of the family celebration on either side, creating the effect of a framed composition. The life upon which he gazes is an idealization of his own past, the repressed late Victorian middle-class world that, as we learn later in the film, ultimately caused the estrangement we are witnessing. In excluding both the viewer and Isak from the luminous security of the interior, Bergman questions that security itself.

Yet there is an important resemblance between Vermeer's images of domestic interiors and those of Bergman. Both artists imagine bourgeois life as architecturally framed. According to the philosopher Gaston Bachelard, human interiority itself is a spatial concept, having to do with our imagination of an "inside," such as the inside of a chest or a drawer. This association is not new; in the ancient world, memory—that most inward of faculties—was conceived of in spatial terms, as ancient techniques of memorization show.[12] In *Either/Or* (1843), Kierkegaard uses the bourgeois interior as a metaphor for the concept of interiority itself; as I have suggested, this metaphor resonates historically. A wide range of scholars have traced parallels between the development of the private home in the seventeenth century and the growth of the inner life of the individual, or "of what we would call a sense of oneself as distinct from that of others and as not fully knowable by others."[13] Thus, Vermeer and Bergman suggest, through different framing devices, the psychological interiority that has increasingly come to be seen as a historical component of bourgeois experience. In *Education of the Senses,* for example, the first volume of Peter Gay's monumental *The Bourgeois Experience: Victoria to Freud,* the historian points to the development of habits of listening in nineteenth-century concert attendance. The inward experience of listening is suggested in both images: in Vermeer, through the gestures of the women (one of whom holds a lute), and in Bergman, through the attentive posture of Isak Borg, played by Victor Sjöstrom.

In both the ghostliness of Bergman's images of the interior and in the vivid presence, in the film, of the typical youth of the new, modern Sweden—the liberated Sara and her two boyfriends—Bergman suggests that the bourgeois domestic world of the nineteenth century is vanishing. In the work of other artists considered here (notably, Dickens, Proust, Benjamin, and Sebald), we also sense the loss of an earlier generation's experience of home. Longing for home is an ancient topos, but its prominence in the novels discussed in these pages may arise from the "transcendental homelessness" that the novel form itself expresses.[14] In the well-known formulation of Georg Lukács, "the problems of the novel form are . . . the mirror-image of a world gone out of joint." The novel's fundamental subject matter is "seeking and failing to find the essence."[15] Stranded Robinson Crusoe, homesick Fanny Price, outcast Oliver Twist and David Copperfield, self-exiled Pip, houseless Fleda Vetch: all face the absence of home and, as a result, conceive of the domestic interior as a space they must reclaim. The bourgeois interior always possesses a trace of nostalgia. In the words of Kierkegaard, its formula is "to feel homesick, even though one is at home."[16] Adapting Lukács's reading of the novel as an estranged form that implicitly alludes to the "totality" and "life-immanence of meaning" of the world of the epic,[17] I suggest that the longing expressed in novels is implicitly for an earlier, more stable middle class, and that this nostalgia is characteristically played out through the medium of the bourgeois interior.

Chapter Review

At the beginning of Defoe's *Robinson Crusoe* (1719), subject of my first chapter, Crusoe's father alludes to this stability in his defense of the "middle state" as a condition his son should seek to emulate. Conceived of in Aristotelian terms as a mean between excess and want, the "middle state" is an ethical ideal that corresponds to a stage in the development of the middle class, which, in comparison with the upward surging bourgeois diaspora that replaced it, occupied a relatively secure position between the extremes of rich and poor. The Dutch Republic of the seventeenth century is the best example of a middle-class society enjoying the "middle state" because of the value the temperamentally conservative cultural milieu of the Dutch placed on rationality and moderation.[18] England in the seventeenth century was beset by violence and revolution, brought to an end in large part by the arrival of the Dutch monarch, William of Orange, in 1688. Crusoe's father, who praises the "middle state," is not from England but Bremen, an autonomous republic until it joined the German Confederation in 1815. In the seventeenth century, when Crusoe's father would have lived there (the period in which capitalism first arose in northern Europe), Bremen was a commanding economic center occupying a strongly fortified position on either side of the Weser. Crusoe is deeply rooted in a solid mercantile middle class.

Robinson Crusoe was published less than fifty years after Vermeer's death and long before the formative stages of industrial capitalism in the early nineteenth century, but the splintering of the middle class into an energetic group of chronically dissatisfied strata between the very wealthy and the working class had already begun.[19] Hints of this development appear in Crusoe's own break with his father, in Pamela's upward mobility in Samuel Richardson's *Pamela* (1740), and, even more emphatically, in the wide economic range of middle-class characters in Austen's fiction. The middle classes of *Emma* (1816) encompass the genteel poverty of Miss Bates and the wealth and grandeur of the Churchills as well as many strata in between. Dickens's later novels fully expose the absence of any notion of a "middle state" among the new middle classes. In *Little Dorrit* (1855–57) and *Our Mutual Friend* (1864–65), for example, consciousness of any stable, moderate social condition has vanished, as characters make merely transitory stopovers between debt and excess.

The elder Crusoe's celebration of the moderate virtues of the middle station in life resonates throughout *Robinson Crusoe.* His son's disobedience and ambition reflect the abandonment of the ethical ideal of the "middle state" by a class enjoying improvements in the standard of living and overcome by the spirit of capitalist enterprise.[20] Crusoe's social isolation and his compulsion to exploit nature and other human beings suggest the loss of humanity that accompanied this spirit. But the ideal of the "middle state" as one of moderation and contentment achieved through the rational satisfaction of wants never leaves Crusoe, who tries (often comically) to recreate it on the island when he builds his enclosure with materials salvaged from the wreck. The earliest bourgeois domestic interior in the English novel is Crusoe's cave, as I have suggested, and it shares with the many bourgeois dwellings to follow an obsession with ownership, security, and the desire to reclaim a more stable prior condition. *Robinson Crusoe* established the paradigm of the bourgeois interior for later writers, and we see in the portrait of Crusoe's "castle" almost all of the essential ingredients of the bourgeoisie's domestic imagination of itself.

In *Persuasion* (1818), Austen comments ironically on this paradigm in the description of Captain Harville's rented lodgings. Austen writes about the gentry or rural bourgeoisie at the moment of its greatest transition. The small preindustrial society of families that Austen knew as a child growing up in the village of Steventon was giving way to a society of individuals, individuals who (paradoxically) would make up the new urban masses. This change is expressed not only through character—for example, in the arrival of those urban individualists, Henry and Mary Crawford, into the rural society of great families in *Mansfield Park* (1814)—but also through domestic space, in a shift of attention from houses to rooms, estates to real estate. Chapter 2 discusses the rented spaces of *Persuasion* and concludes with a close analysis of Fanny Price's room in *Mansfield Park* and of the ambivalent objects in it. In treating Fanny's unhappy visit to the urban dwelling of her parents, it also considers the place of nostalgia in the bourgeois imagination of home.

Fanny's deep identification with and attachment to the objects in her room at Mansfield and her homesickness for the Mansfield estate when she is in Portsmouth prefigure what

Benjamin called the nineteenth-century "addiction to dwelling," my subject in chapter 3, which takes up Dickens's novels. According to Benjamin, in the nineteenth century the interior became something more than "just the universe of the private individual"; it became his "étui," the protective cover designed to shield him from the shocks of urban life.[21] (In his later essay on Baudelaire, Benjamin relates the protective impulse to Freud's characterization of consciousness as a screen that resists the force of traumatic memory.[22]) In postindustrial society, Benjamin's bourgeois attempts "to compensate for the absence of any trace of private life in the big city. He tries to do this within the four walls of his apartment. It is as if he had made it a point of honor not to allow the traces of his everyday objects and accessories to get lost."[23] Behind his étui, the screen or cushion provided by his domestic interior and its objects, the bourgeois seeks and finds his identity—or, more precisely, seeks and finds and seeks again the self that eludes him, as in a game of hide-and-seek.

Chapter 3 begins with a discussion of Dickens's pursuit of the bourgeois domestic ideal both in his fiction and in his personal life. As regards the latter, it characterizes Dickens's failed attempt to establish Urania Cottage, a home for rehabilitated prostitutes, as an effort to bring about a kind of shotgun wedding between the domestic ideal and modern society. I draw parallels between Urania Cottage and David Copperfield's entrance into bourgeois space at Dover: in both cases, the socially degraded self must be effaced. In this chapter, Miss Havisham's house in *Great Expectations* (1861) is treated as a paradigm of the Victorian home as fortress, prison, and tomb, but also as a "transparency" through which Pip sees into his past; as both a material and immaterial space, the interior of Satis House penetrates the barrier between reality and dream. The interiors of the Meagleses (*Little Dorrit*) and the Boffins (*Our Mutual Friend*) are also examined for what they reveal about the commodity-laden mentality of the late Victorian middle class, and the chapter ends with a section entitled "The Beloved Object and the Commodity," in which I consider the transformation of the treasured objects of the earlier novels into the junk heaps of the later ones.

Chapter 4 further explores the different ways people of the late nineteenth century related to objects—both "real" people, like William Morris and Henry James, and fictional characters, or those in James's novella about the human attachment to things, *The Spoils of Poynton.* Beginning with the chapter on James, my selection of literary texts by individual authors narrows. Coming after the classic novelists of domestic space treated in chapters 1 through 3, James, Woolf, Updike, and Sebald write much more self-consciously about the bourgeois interior, as if, in particular works, they are in conversation with their predecessors and contemporaries on the subject. "What, finally, are 'things'?" James seems to ask. "What, finally, is 'home'?" queries Woolf.

In its discussion of the three interiors in *The Spoils of Poynton*—the comically disgusting Waterbath, the "perfect" collection of Poynton, and the resonant and redemptive interior of the deceased aunt—chapter 4 considers different kinds of fetishism. It aims to recover an earlier notion of the fetish (one that predates Marx's and Freud's appropriation of the term) in its discussion of James's attribution of life to inanimate things. In breaking with the tradition of nineteenth-century realism, James had to free himself from what he called the "smell" of things: their vulgar association with the "machinery of life . . . its furniture and fittings."[24] He seems to have done this by opening himself to their "spell": their magical aura, their capacity to embody the essence of human thought and feeling and to penetrate the levels of time by bringing the past into the present. This chapter also places James's attention to late Victorian taste, to fetishism and collecting, in the context of nineteenth-century controversies about taste and value, controversies from which James was beginning to distance himself. However one interprets the conflagration at the end of the story, its vision of the domestic interior is marked by a savage sense of loss, both human and material. As Victoria Rosner suggests, it is almost as if the Victorian home in James's story were "unable to survive the passage to modernity."[25]

Howards End, in E. M. Forster's 1910 novel by that name, does survive the transition to modernity but not without sacrificing its bourgeois character. At the end of *Howards End,* an unconventional family has replaced the traditional family that once inhabited the domestic interior. In Virginia Woolf's *To the Lighthouse* (1927), subject of chapter 5, a house deteriorates with the death of the Victorian mother, Mrs. Ramsey, and the world is reimagined by an unmarried woman artist who lives in rooms in London that we never see. The bourgeois home as mythological configuration is coming to an end. While the bourgeois class continued in full force, the domestic interior was being reconceived by the antibourgeois energies of Bloomsbury as well as by the modernist architecture of Le Corbusier, whose writings first appeared in the 1920s. One of the main points of this chapter is that with changes in the status of women, the type of Victorian womanhood represented by Mrs. Ramsey (and epitomized by Woolf's mother, upon whom Mrs. Ramsey is based) receded from the cultural stage; with her departure, Victorian domesticity foundered. Neither Forster nor Woolf imagines a future for bourgeois domesticity, and Woolf intimates that, without housewives to humanize the home, domesticity itself would not survive, at least in forms familiar to her culture. The power of our *memory* of Victorian domesticity then becomes an important subject in both literature and film.

To word this another way: If the nineteenth-century interior had acted as a protective screen, in much the same way that consciousness shields the subject from traumatic memory, it follows that the demise of the Victorian interior should result in an explosion of memory. In chapter 6, which considers the films of Ingmar Bergman, I argue that through the art of film, and particularly in films made after the greatest works of high modernism by Proust, Joyce, Woolf, and others had made their impact, a dazzling treatment of the bourgeois interior as the medium of memory and dream emerges. The sense of loss that characterizes visions of the interior in both *Wild Strawberries* and *Fanny and Alexander* (1982) takes us beyond the revaluations of memory in Dickens that influenced Bergman and beyond the openly ambivalent engagement with the past in Woolf and Forster into emotions that are more purely elegiac. This is true as well in a work that *Fanny and Alexander* echoes, Benjamin's *Berlin Childhood around 1900*.[26] Both Benjamin and Bergman seem to be bidding farewell not simply to a certain kind of bourgeois experience but to the interiors in which that experience was inscribed. The example of Proust, who also memorializes the spaces and customs of the bourgeois world in *Remembrance of Things Past* (1913–27), is vital to both artists. In Bergman, the bourgeois interior is once again a medium through which cultural forces are acting, causing it to change from generation to generation at the same time that it retains its domestic character. One of the consummate achievements in a genre that is normally associated with American film, that of the "road movie," *Wild Strawberries* attests to the durability of the image of the domestic interior in artworks set in a transient society. Even in the homeless universe of W. G. Sebald, discussed briefly in the conclusion to this work, the tradition of the domestic interior in fiction is drawn on to explore the often inconspicuous devastations of the present. After considering a short story by John Updike, I end with a discussion of Sebald's "Dr Henry Selwyn," the first story in *The Emigrants* (1997), because in it we see the full development of the bourgeois isolation of Robinson Crusoe, to which Sebald may be alluding. Echoes of interiors in earlier English fiction are vital to both Updike's and Sebald's stories, suggesting their awareness of the inextinguishable energy of the domestic interior as memory and image, even (or above all) in the transient context of the modern world.

Contemporary theorists of bourgeois domestic space tend to view the interior in a critical light: they see it as designed to "valorize the bourgeois subject" and to promote the socially assigned roles of businessman, wife, and mother.[27] This book does not necessarily contradict this judgment, although my focus on literary texts suggests that the bourgeois interior is more alive and comic, more resonant and mysterious, than most theoretical readings have allowed. Two exceptionally rich studies that have appeared recently—Diana Fuss's *The Sense of an Interior: Four Writers and the Rooms that Shaped Them* and Victoria Rosner's *Modernism and the Architecture of Private Life*—suggest that research on the domestic interior is moving away from a more political to a more literary perspective.[28] Although their studies do not concentrate on the bourgeois interior per se, they have enriched my own readings.

Many contemporary readings of the bourgeois interior—and my own is no exception—are indebted to the work of Walter Benjamin, yet few seem to acknowledge, as I believe this study does, Benjamin's ambivalence toward the bourgeoisie. In *Berlin Childhood around 1900,* Benjamin writes with loving, Proustian detail about the bourgeois interior of his childhood; he never forgot that he himself was rooted in the bourgeoisie, and he collected the letters in *German Men and Women* (1931–32) out of a desire to honor the preindustrial bourgeois class of his native country. In the latter work, Benjamin identifies the domestic interior of an earlier era as a uniquely human space. Although Benjamin has shown us more than any other author how the nineteenth-century bourgeois interior colludes with the social forces of capitalism, he also recognized the domestic interior as the refuge and theater of imaginative life for the bourgeois individual (and especially the child of the bourgeois class), a mimetic *spielraum* or space for play in the profoundest sense. To say that "the interior is the place where society manufactures desocialization," as one critic puts it,[29] is therefore somewhat one-sided, since the interior is also the place where the bourgeois tries to compensate for his desocialization or to counterbalance and fend off his alienation. It is a masquerade in a double sense, negative and positive.

To take an example: The nineteenth-century fashion of panoramic wallpaper depicting mythological stories, classical antiquities, the English countryside, and colonial encounters has been variously interpreted as an effort to efface the boundary created by the wall and project oneself out of the world and history, and as an attempt to represent England's "grammar of empire."[30] Yet it may also be seen as an aesthetic effort to situate oneself *in* history or to feel coextensive with a world in which one senses one's own insignificance.[31] This effort may have been a "point of honor" to the bourgeois man who gazed on the panorama, however vainly (in both senses of the word), and it may have been a point of honor to the bourgeois woman who did so as well, although her relations to the domestic interior were no doubt different from those of her husband. Her "bias for settlement" may have owed something to the desire for fixity she may have experienced during periods of child-rearing, a desire that need not be characterized as "bourgeois through and through." In other words, the reasonableness of this desire is not negated by the fact that the holders of power, in denying the public access to information about birth control, were intent on confining women to the home.

Nineteenth-century novels are of course full of powerful renderings of dwelling that undermine too simple a view of the bourgeois dweller. One example will have to serve. In George Eliot's *Middlemarch* (1871–72), the domestic interior arranged by Lydgate and his wife Rosamond, with its fine plate, bibelots, and heavy furniture, is the most pretentious dwelling in the novel, a place where the couple seems almost to have staged a "refusal to be somewhere"[32]—to use Didier Maleuve's phrase for the bourgeois experience of dwelling—for they view their furnishings as one of the indications of their superiority to the provincial society in which they live. Yet at crucial narrative junctures, Eliot's narrator pauses to envision Lydgate as he returns to his bourgeois paradise, now the site of tension and misery:

> It was evening when he got home. He was intensely miserable, this strong man of nine-and-twenty and of many gifts.
>
> He got down from his horse in a very sad mood, and went into the house, not expecting to be cheered except by his dinner.[33]

In these rueful images of homecoming, Eliot does not allow us to forget the human need to dwell. If the nineteenth-century "interior dweller dwells in homelessness," he dwells nonetheless.[34]

Some studies of the bourgeois interior, like those I have cited earlier, are interested in collapsing entirely the separation between the home and the world, whereas my study collapses it only partially. One reason for preserving the distinction is the relative privacy and security of the English middle-class home in comparison with the dwellings of those beneath the middle class, including those in the colonies. Homi K. Bhabha identifies what he calls "the unhomely" as "a paradigmatic postcolonial experience": "The unhomely is the shock of recognition of the world-in-the-home, the home-in-the-world" that often accompanies the lives of the poor and disenfranchised in novels by V. S. Naipaul, Nadine Gordimer, Toni Morrison, and others.[35] Can these "freak displacements" in which "the outsideness of the inside"[36] is suddenly and painfully made manifest be placed on the same level with the bourgeois alienation from home reflected in Austen, Balzac, or Dickens? To return this distinction to the life of Walter Benjamin: There is a difference between the homeless circumstances of his death in Spain as he tried to escape the Nazis and the *illusion of security* created by the bourgeois interiors he wrote about and inhabited—a difference that does not preclude a connection. One may explore such connections by applying the critique of other institutions to the houses of the bourgeoisie, as critics have done in treating the home as a microcosm of the museum, the department store, and the body politic, but the distinctions among institutions deserve consideration as well.

We have only to think of the impersonality of so many architectural spaces of the postindustrial world, such as airports, courts of law, and banks, to see that the distinctions between the domestic interior and other locations are significant. As Austerlitz comments in W. G. Sebald's novel by that name: "Someone . . . ought to draw up a catalogue of the types of buildings listed in order of size, and it would be immediately obvious that domestic buildings of *less* than normal size . . . are those that offer us at least a semblance of peace, whereas no one in his right mind could truthfully say that he liked a vast edifice such as the Palace of Justice on the old Gallows Hill in Brussels."[37] *Illusions of security, semblances of peace.* Perhaps I show the influence of Sebald's more chilling meditations on modern architecture when I suggest that the domestic interior wears a human face, one that is no less human for being a mask.

The Bourgeois Soul

Oscar Wilde once asked of a friend whether he had ever been known to "take off his face and reveal his mask."[38] The bourgeois reveals himself through his mask, through the things he feels he needs that are "superfluous." I take the word *superfluous* from one of the most eloquent defenses ever written of the human need for a protective mask or étui: King Lear's response to Regan when she asks him why he must keep knights in attendance:

> O reason not the need. Our basest beggars
> Are in the poorest thing superfluous.
> Allow not nature more than nature needs,
> Man's life is cheap as beast's.[39]

Lear speaks for high and low alike when he defends the human need for more than what is strictly necessary. In taking as its subject the concerns of the middle class, this study moves away from the extremes of tragedy, yet Lear's generous words apply to the bourgeois as well, not least because of that very quality that distinguishes the bourgeois from the tragic figure: his characteristic unwillingness to expose himself to suffering. The bourgeois craves security and longs for what Nietzsche called "green-pasture happiness,"[40] even when, like Lydgate, his bourgeois desires debilitate him. When adversity arrives, he meets his fate: "the pathos of a lot where everything is below the level of tragedy except the passionate egoism of the sufferer."[41]

Solipsistic egoism is constantly before the novelist's gaze and—with a few notable exceptions like *David Copperfield*—is generally resisted. Into Robinson Crusoe's first-person narrative Defoe inserts droll contradictions; Austen's narrator chastises egoism with irony; Dickens's "unpsychological and illustrative method" of characterization undermines an individualistic psychology;[42] George Eliot's plot configurations, by which characters get what they thought they wanted, devastate characters' egos: all of these techniques serve to challenge the point of view of the bourgeois. But it is in the realistic depiction of the object-world—specifically, the object-world of the domestic interior—that the novelist's resistance to bourgeois subjectivity is at its most ambivalent. For this is the bourgeois' own world of things, and it therefore faces both ways: inward toward the self and outward toward the world at large. The very objects within the interior, as if alive, quietly resist the psychological inwardness they reinforce. As Theodor Adorno suggests in his critique of Kierkegaard's use of the bourgeois interior as a metaphor for subjectivity itself, the "objective, historical contents" of the interior effortlessly challenge the philosopher's apparently individualistic intention.[43] The objects in the interior are figments of the bourgeois imagination, elements of a world he has dreamt up, at the same time that they are palpable presences with a historical and economic determination all their own, and a final destiny as trash. In this way, the domestic interior becomes the site of a subtle tug-of-war for the bourgeois soul itself. Bergman's arresting image of Isak Borg prompts us to pose a question that will appear more than once in these pages: does the interior haunt the bourgeois or does the bourgeois, like a ghost, haunt the interior?

Robinson Crusoe's Cave

The first bourgeois interior in English fiction is located in a cave. Every reader remembers Robinson Crusoe's carefully constructed domestic enclosure, with its handcrafted table and chair and its inventory of useful objects arranged on shelves. Published in 1719, *Robinson Crusoe* is regarded by many as the first English novel. Not least among its achievements is its prophecy of the radical alteration our relations to domestic space would undergo with the rise of capitalist enterprise and ownership. Crusoe's inventory of domestic objects is the first in a line of such inventories that extends through many nineteenth-century novels to the Ithaca chapter in James Joyce's *Ulysses,* where Leopold Bloom enumerates the objects that would fill the bourgeois home of his imagination. The concept of home as the locus of *things* is found in realist and nonrealist fiction alike, as well as in works that draw on both traditions, such as those of Joyce and Sebald.

Many other aspects of Crusoe's domestic fortress set the stage for later images of the bourgeois home: the home as fortress, first of all; the strong association between the home and private property; the role of the domestic arts in the home, which Virginia Woolf may have been the first to observe;[1] the place of the servant who lives within but sleeps apart from the family (Friday's bed is made up outside of Crusoe's cave, just as, later in history when domestic technology replaced servants, labor-saving devices would be hidden from view); the problematic role of the family in the individualist psychology of the capitalist (Crusoe keeps pets, but could we ever imagine him with a family?); the place of the second home as refuge from the first; and, not unrelated to the latter phenomenon, the bourgeois home as the expression of a desire to reclaim a prior condition of stability or contentment. The list goes on.[2]

Fittingly, *Robinson Crusoe* begins with a lengthy eulogy to the "middle state" delivered by the hero's father. This statement recalls Aristotle's original exposition of the merits of the middle constitution within the larger framework of his *Politics.* There, Aristotle had outlined the inherent benefits of a middle class to the vitality of society as a whole, as well as to middle-station citizens themselves, who enjoy the security of a stable, moderate way of life that citizens of higher and lower stations are unlikely to achieve.[3] Crusoe's father echoes Aristotle as he expostulates with his son on the life of adventure his son contemplates:

> He ask'd me what Reasons more than a mere wandering Inclination I had for leaving my Father's House and my native Country, where I . . . had a Prospect of raising my Fortune by Application and Industry, with a Life of Ease and Pleasure. He told me . . . that these things were all either too far above me, or too far below me; that mine was the middle State . . . which he had found by long Experience was the best State in the World, the most suited to human Happiness, not exposed to the Miseries and Hardships, the Labour and Sufferings of the mechanick Part of Mankind, and not embarrassed with Pride, Luxury, Ambition, and Envy of the upper Part of Mankind. He told me I might judge of the Happiness of this State by this one thing, *viz.* That this was the State of Life which all other People envied. . . . that Peace and Plenty . . . Temperance, Moderation . . . and all desirable Pleasures, were the Blessings attending the middle Station of Life.[4]

This passage makes clear not only what Crusoe abandons but also what he subsequently longs for and *thinks* he wants. Crusoe's disobedience to his father sets the plot going and hints at the evacuation of the middle state by the middle class that later novelists will expose more fully. In Defoe's novel, however, the middle state is too much a part of the hero's consciousness for him to relinquish it entirely. Stranded on the island, Crusoe strives to attain as comfortable and safe an existence as any middle-class Englishman could desire. There at last, after years of discontented wandering, he is able by means of "application and industry" to moderate his wants according to his needs. At the end of four years he can boast that he has attained exactly the degree of rational satisfaction that his father had insisted all other classes envied: "I had nothing to covet; for I had all that I was now capable of enjoying. . . . The most covetous griping Miser in the World would have been cured of the Vice of Covetousness, if he had been in my Case."[5]

Crusoe's statement of satisfaction and the passage in which it is placed establish a pattern in the novel in which the hero, at regular intervals, announces the year of his residence on the island, enumerates the goods he has acquired or crafted, and finally describes in detail the improvements and additions to his dwelling. The action of the novel pauses—Crusoe literally stops work—as he boasts of his achievement of the middle-class goals recommended by his father, that "State of Life which all other People envied."[6] The problem, of course, is that Crusoe is never satisfied. Ideally situated for a *surplus* of goods to seem a *necessity*—who that found himself helplessly stranded on a remote island could ever feel that his stock of goods was too great?—he immediately turns his attention to acquiring or building more.

John E. Crowley's illuminating discussion of changing ideas of necessity and luxury in early modern Britain emphasizes the importance of *Robinson Crusoe* to "the invention of comfort" or to the development of "a new language to describe the physical basis of material need." Where in earlier periods, the word *luxury* referred to a condition in excess of what necessity required, the development of political economy in the eighteenth century "made it possible for both *luxury* and *necessity* to become morally neutral terms." A new, somewhat ambiguous notion of comfort emerges, and Defoe's novel promotes it, Crowley argues. Whereas in principle "comfort implicitly involved knowing what amenities one really needed, having them, and desiring no more," *Robinson Crusoe* repeatedly contradicts this "simple equation of comfort with the satisfaction of sheer necessities" because of the way Crusoe's needs keep expanding.[7] As the standard of living rose, middle-class "needs" increased. Indeed, history has repeatedly shown that one generation's "luxury" (whether it be central heating, electricity, or the telephone) becomes the next generation's "necessity."

The greed Crusoe eventually confesses to having displayed in his illegal slave expedition is implicitly legitimized by his stranded circumstances. "I possess'd infinitely more than I knew what to do with," he remarks. How necessary to the "Stock of all Necessaries," for example, are the fifteen great wicker baskets stored in the cave?[8] Crusoe will not be the last bourgeois to discover that he has achieved contentment only to have it undermined by the inextinguishable desire for more. Ultimately, what Crusoe desires is a state of mind free from desire: the middle state of mind praised by his father.

Bourgeois security is further undermined by the constant vigilance required to sustain it. In the first few years on the island Crusoe builds and furnishes his enclosure: "a tent under the side of a rock, surrounded with a strong pale of posts and cables" that eventually grows into a thick wall of trees. Rafters covered with boughs of trees protect him from the rain, and he enlarges the interior of the cave to make room for the many goods salvaged from the ship. After securing this shelter, he goes to work to make a table and chair, and to become "Master of every mechanick Art" necessary to furnishing his new home. Crusoe seems satisfied with the result. His habitation, he proudly observes, "looked like a general Magazine of all Necessary things, and I had everything so ready at my hand, that it was a great Pleasure to me to see all my Goods in such

Order, and especially to find my Stock of all Necessaries so great."[9]

The pride and pleasure Crusoe takes in his inventory, however, go hand in hand with an intense anxiety to protect it. After he sees the footprint, he creates a double wall around the enclosure for greater security and increases the thickness of the inside wall to ten feet. Musquets are planted through holes in the inside wall, arranged so that he can fire all seven in two minutes' time. "This Wall I was many a weary Month a finishing, and yet never thought my self safe till it was done." Still dissatisfied after completing it, however, Crusoe proceeds to create yet a third wall of stakes, leaving a large space between them and the second wall "that I might have room to see an Enemy, and they might have no shelter from the young Trees, if they attempted to approach my outer Wall. . . . Thus in two Years Time I had a thick Grove, and in five or six Years time I had Wood before my Dwelling, growing so monstrous thick and strong, that it was indeed perfectly impassable."[10] Crusoe's pride in his "castle" is evident in the loving detail with which he describes the unending effort to secure it. In time, he never emerges from his enclosure without his umbrella and his gun, symbols of his respectability and his violence.

Crusoe's attitude toward his dwelling is a peculiar combination of pride and paranoia: pride and pleasure in what he has created combined with a constant waking fear that it will be wrested from him. The eighteenth century saw an increase in the design, building, and improvement of military fortifications, especially the immense star-shaped fortress. W. G. Sebald meditates on this phenomenon in *Austerlitz:* as "intent as everyone was on [the star-shaped] pattern, it had been forgotten that the largest fortifications will naturally attract the largest enemy forces, and that the more you entrench yourself the more you must remain on the defensive. . . . The frequent result . . . of resorting to measures of fortification marked in general by a tendency toward paranoid elaboration was that you drew attention to your weakest point, practically inviting the enemy to attack it."[11] Crusoe comes to regret the "paranoid elaboration" of his dwelling years later when he realizes the danger of attack from cannibals: "Now I began to repent, that I had dug my Cave so large, as to bring a Door through again, which . . . came out beyond where my fortification [ended]," he comments as he desperately tries to make the area appear as natural as possible.[12] If, at any rate, we take the bourgeois interior as an index of the mental state of the bourgeois, then Crusoe's cave, with its cozy comfort, its well-placed shelves and objects, and above all its elaborate security system prefigures many bourgeois dwellings to follow. His description of the fail-safe alarm system by which the sight of the enemy outside the enclosure triggers a series of chain reactions within brings to mind expensive security systems designed today, in which hidden cameras are set up to view intruders and burglar alarms go off simultaneously in private houses and local police stations.

How can one feel at home in such a "prison"—a word that Crusoe himself uses to describe his dwelling side by side with the word *castle*? By creating a second home to which one may retreat and view the first at a distance: another prophetic dimension of Crusoe's bourgeois domain. It is only after he creates his "Country-House" that Crusoe begins to call his tent and cave "Home."[13] To feel homelike, or to be experienced subjectively as safely familiar, a dwelling must be objectified as a haven to which one may return. The second home makes this possible. After a month at his Country-House, Crusoe is "very impatient to be at Home. . . . I cannot express what a satisfaction it was to me to come into my old Hutch, and lye down in my Hamock-bed."[14] Crusoe's Country-House, like many a later one, is more open and inviting than his main dwelling; he refers to it as his "Bower," and the inevitable protective fence that surrounds it is located "at a Distance."[15] Crusoe is never so secure as when he is outside his fortification, dreaming of its security.[16]

Essential to the potentially violent spirit of protectiveness inspired by his main dwelling—"I was in a murthering Humour," admits Crusoe after he sees the cannibals invade the island—is of course the conviction of ownership.[17] The fortification, the land, the island itself: all belong to Crusoe. Just as he never questions his right to property over that of the tribe of savages who have been coming to its shore for years, perhaps centuries, Crusoe judges his habitation and everything in it to be rightfully his and his alone. Yet the majority of his possessions are salvaged from the wreck, and one could argue that the entire supply of merchandise displayed in his "magazine" is stolen. While his desperate circumstances as a castaway forestall the reader's disapproval, the "wishful affirmation of a flagrant economic naiveté—the idea that anyone has ever attained comfort and security entirely by his own efforts"—is felt on every page of the novel.[18] It is *effort* that makes Crusoe feel that he is "lord of the whole manor . . . king or emperor over the whole country which [he] had possession of."[19] The care with which he crafts his table and chair, extends day into night when he makes the candle, builds an enclosure for his goats, and through steady determination finally creates a clay cooking pot makes it seem only natural that he should proudly claim these things as his own property. To capture, train, and enslave another human being and claim proprietary rights over an entire island (as Crusoe does later when others arrive) appear to be the natural extensions of a conviction of private ownership, and Crusoe describes these actions with the same methodical attention to planning and execution that characterizes his construction of his interior space.

Crusoe proceeds by a logic of personal right and self-aggrandizement that most readers of first-person narrative, with its amoral capacity for identification, are insufficiently distanced from to question. After having been rescued from death by Crusoe, Friday humbly offers thanks by laying his head on the ground close to Crusoe's foot, frantically making gestures that, according to Crusoe, are aimed "to let me know how, he would serve me as long as he liv'd."[20] Certain physical gestures of submission, such as the bending of the neck or the placing of the head under the victor's foot, are identifiable across cultures, but what is the gesture that could communicate servitude over time, servitude in perpetuity? Coolly enumerating his schemes of human and material acquisition to the last page of the novel, Crusoe describes how he allocates land to future settlers of the island while "reserv[ing] to my self the Property of the whole." With characteristic generosity as well as unconscious irony, he augments their claims: "besides other Supplies, I sent seven Women."[21]

The reader is of course distracted from contemplating the more egregious instances of Crusoe's possessiveness and aggression by the religious allegory, derived from John Bunyan, of man's isolation before God, an allegory that Crusoe himself is slow to embrace. When he first arrives on the island, the natural environment possesses for him a radical otherness, such that he cannot even name the things he sees and must settle for approximations: "a thick bushy Tree like a Firr," "a Kind of Hawk," "a Creature like a wild Cat," and so on.[22] The island resists comprehension by language, and Crusoe's physical efforts encounter a similar intractability. He spends five days trying to make a chair, "pull[ing] it to Pieces several times" in frustration.[23] As nature resists civilization, she risks being destroyed:

> [At] my coming back, I shot at a great Bird which I saw sitting upon a Tree on the Side of a great Wood; I believe it was the first Gun that had been fir'd there since the Creation of the World; I had no sooner fir'd, but from all the Parts of the Wood there arose innumerable Number of Fowls of many Sorts, making a confus'd Screaming, and crying every one according to his usual Note; but not one of them of any Kind that I knew: As for the Creature I kill'd, I took it to be a Kind of Hawk, its Colour and Beak resembling it, but had no Talons or Claws more than common, its Flesh was Carrion and fit for nothing.[24]

This passage hints at a materialist assault on a traditional, religious understanding of nature. English scientists of the seventeenth century, like Francis Bacon, worked to reveal a divinely ordained pattern in nature. In *The New Atlantis,* Bacon envisions a perfect society dedicated to scientific investigation that will lead to the perfection of man. Diseases will be cured, for example, returning human beings to the perfect health they enjoyed in the Garden of Eden. Science and technology will perfect nature through invention. In *Robinson Crusoe,* technology, represented above all in the barrels of gun powder, seems to be doing the reverse: destroying natural objects in the drive to find their utility for man. At the beginning of Crusoe's stay on the island, nature is not God's Book, as it had been called by scientists like Bacon and Robert Boyle or poets like John Donne and John Milton, but a harsh, intractable, unnamable substance "fit for nothing." For this reason, the religious narrative of *Robinson Crusoe* takes on an entirely subjective, personal cast. God, whose sole client seems to be the hero, has forsaken the world of nature and even that of other men, such as the tribe of cannibals, "whom Heaven had thought fit . . . to suffer unpunish'd," remarks Crusoe.[25] Again and again, Crusoe reminds us that his "Providence" is someone else's disaster, and he frequently benefits when others suffer or are killed. Crusoe's parrot, which he characterizes as family, elicits more emotion from him than the corpse of a drowned boy that provides him with a tobacco pipe, "of ten times more value than the. . . . two Pieces of Eight" in the dead boy's pocket.[26] The wry humor that often accompanies these instances of Crusoe's opportunism is more likely to inspire in the reader a curl of the lip than outright laughter. Details such as these, at any rate, are what make it impossible for us to imagine Crusoe with a human family.

Because Crusoe has such difficulty altering the natural environment to suit his purposes, he resorts to altering the way he describes it instead. During and after his terrible illness, despair forces a religious conversion and the inevitable conclusion that words can have both concrete and symbolic significance: "Now I began to construe the Words . . . *Call on me and I will deliver you* in a different Sense from what I had ever done before." No longer praying for deliverance from the island, he now prays for deliverance from sin: "I learn'd to take [the word] in another Sense."[27] Once Crusoe is able to think in allegorical terms, the island appears more familiar to him. He discovers a fruitful Eden in its center that looks "like a planted Garden";[28] as a Christian, he has come into man's estate at last. Species are no longer strange—one of his cats miraculously breeds with an animal on the island—and Crusoe begins to name birds precisely when he refers to "*Penguins.*"[29] Yet even as the island loses its radical otherness to become the site of Christian allegory, Defoe never abandons attention to the discrepancy between things and the ideas Crusoe has of them, frequently suggesting the distinction in double references like "the Hole in the Rock, which I call'd a Door" and "Apartments, or Caves."[30] The most striking instance of this takes place in the building of the boat from a tree trunk that is too heavy to get into the water. The "tree" never does become a "boat" and rots on shore as a testimony to the disjunction between things and the words we attach to them.

After his conversion, Crusoe becomes a paragon of the human species, producing one invention after another. His labor mimics a recapitulation of human development in nature, from a primitive stage of naked subsistence, to agricultural and religious stages (which occur at the same time, as Crusoe's first religious feeling is born with the seemingly miraculous growing of corn), to the recapturing of art (he makes the pot), the semantic stage (the parrot talks), and so on.[31] All of this attention to Universal Man serves to veil Bourgeois Man, for in addition to his symbolic material development, Crusoe has looted a ship in order to recreate an English "estate" on foreign soil, replete with "Livestock," a "Castle," and a "Country-House."[32] The degree to which he has abandoned his father's ideal of the "middle state" is nowhere more prominently displayed than in his self-description as "Lord of the whole Manor," which, with comic obtuseness, he delivers just after he claims that he has been cured of pride.[33]

The wreck stands for Crusoe's past life, for memory itself, and the description of its looting possesses profound energy. As J. M. Coetzee writes, "when Crusoe has to solve the hundreds of little practical problems involved in getting the contents of the ship ashore . . . one can feel the writing move into higher gear, a more intense level of engagement."[34] Returning again and again to the wreck, rummaging through barrels and chests, hoisting objects over the ship's side, loading them onto a raft, Crusoe robs the ship of almost everything in it of value. Symbolically, the past is being dismantled, stripped, and destroyed so that Crusoe can live off its ruins.

Starting with his father's emigration from Bremen and the family's Anglicization of their name, Crusoe's family has a history of severing itself from the past. Like the Prodigal Son, Crusoe himself breaks with his father; but, unlike the father in the parable, the elder Crusoe never learns what became of his son, as Crusoe himself matter-of-factly tells us. (Friday's reunion with his father offers a stark contrast.) In a sense, the name *Crusoe* is looted from *Kreutznaer*—that is, the new name is appropriated, ripped out of context, like the objects taken from the wreck. For Crusoe, the present does not emerge naturally out of the past but is wrested from it, leaving only a husk to be discarded. After thoroughly ransacking the ship, Crusoe awakens one morning to find it has vanished. Symbolically, the implications of its disappearance are chilling—if you desecrate your past you will lose it—but they are not fully explored until much later in history, as we shall see in the discussion of W. G. Sebald. It is too simple, at any rate, to see *Robinson Crusoe* as "unabashed propaganda for the extension of British mercantile power in the New World and the establishment of new British colonies,"[35] as critics today have done, because the novel contains too many hints of a destructive daemon shadowing the Protestant Mercantile-God that Crusoe worships. On route to

Cape Verde early in the novel, Crusoe shoots a "mighty Creature" as it plunges and plays in the sea, murdering it primarily to divert the surrounding natives. After firing his gun "directly into the Head," he watches it die as it struggles for air. Later, he hunts for the carcass: "I found him by his Blood staining the Water . . . a most curious Leopard, spotted and fine to an admirable Degree, and the *Negroes* held up their Hands with Admiration to think what it was I had kill'd him with."[36] The dialectical thrust of this sentence turns on the self-negating repetition in the words *admirable* and *admiration.* The leopard's beauty is admired together with the power that destroys it.

The naming of Friday is another such instance of veiled contradiction. As critics have noted, Crusoe does not ask Friday his name, he gives him one, a gesture that may be read simply as another instance of that "unabashed propaganda" on behalf of British imperialism. But a curious equivocation accompanies the naming of Friday. Culminating the elaborate pattern of giving familiar names to unfamiliar phenomena in the novel, the naming of Friday boomerangs just as Crusoe's effort to turn the tree trunk into a boat had backfired. At the end of his adventure on the island, Crusoe learns that the calendar that he has been keeping for decades is inaccurate, which means of course that Friday, named for the day he was found, is misnamed. Such sardonic undercurrents complicate the colonialist enterprise of Robinson Crusoe, even if they do not undermine it. The epigraph of Sebald's "Dr Henry Selwyn" would be an appropriate epitaph for Crusoe: "*And the last remnants / memory destroys.*"[37] Whatever is left of the past, after one has renounced it, will be destroyed by the memory of what one has done—if one has a memory. From the early pages of the novel, when Crusoe repeatedly forgets the "Vows . . . made in [his] Distress," to his frustration at not remembering how to make bread, to later exclamations about the "Chequer-Work of Providence" by which "To Day we love what to Morrow we hate,"[38] Crusoe never tires of reminding us of his poor memory. But in composing a document of written memory to compensate for this weakness, Crusoe (and Defoe) leave a record of what capitalist man might otherwise have forgotten.

From its origins in English fiction in Defoe's novel, the bourgeois domestic interior is associated with memory. In building his enclosure, Crusoe draws on memory to replicate the spaces he has known in the past. And while his recollections are not presented as the self-conscious acts of revaluation and inward exploration that we see in such later novelists as Dickens and Proust, the novel contains a striking declaration about memory—"that great thorow-fare of the Brain," as Crusoe calls it[39]—and Crusoe's enclosure as memory-space resonates historically. In *The Art of Memory,* Frances Yates writes of the ancient association of memory and place and of how the great memory theaters of the Renaissance influenced the rise of science. Originating as a method derived from the Greeks for memorizing the encyclopedia of knowledge, the memory theater of Camillo and the system of memory of Bruno became an aid for *investigating* that encyclopedia with the aim of discovering new knowledge.[40] In *Robinson Crusoe,* Defoe places emphasis on memory as both an ordering principle and a tool that facilitates invention, investigation, and classification. The domestic interior becomes the site of this double use of memory, the place where Crusoe both "looks back" and "sees before" (the literal meaning of the word *providence,* that great motivating principle of the plot). In this way the objects in his interior are repositories of both the past and future. The wicker baskets stored in the interior of the cave are symbols of the past—he creates them by drawing on boyhood memories of watching village craftsmen make them—as well as of the future, which they quite literally "hold."

Like that of the bourgeois of succeeding generations, Crusoe's profoundest relationship is to things. His internal religious monologue, his exchanges with Friday, his final rescue and return to civilization: none attain the level of inner exhilaration inspired by the finding, crafting, and ordering of things for his enclosure. Because his loneliness arises not from geo-

A recently "resurfaced" medieval-style fortress in Orlando, Florida, complete with a three-car garage and Christmas lights. As Benjamin observed, the middle classes "will never quite have done with feudalism." (Courtesy of Howard Eiland)

graphic isolation but from the restless nature of the bourgeois mental utopia he inhabits—the inventory of things—he is off wandering again at the end of the novel, abandoning his comfortable life in civilization as he had earlier abandoned his Brazil plantation. When Thomas Babington Macaulay remarked on the peculiarity of *Robinson Crusoe*—"the strange union of comfort, plenty, and security with the misery of loneliness"[41] —he unwittingly stumbled on the very essence of bourgeois life. Sexually repressed or indifferent (women are no more than "supplies"), intent on using other human beings as servants, fixated on securing and enlarging his territory, the bourgeois capitalist does not elicit great emotion. His fate is like that of the novel itself, as Dickens described it: "*Robinson Crusoe* [is] the only instance of an universally popular book that could make no one laugh and could make no one cry."[42]

Nonetheless, the description of Crusoe's early years on the island possesses enormous appeal, and one that is more complicated than the pleasure we feel in simply imagining a supreme adventure. For in spite of the fact that Crusoe's accomplishments are unrealistic (as accounts of other castaways who were reduced to far more primitive conditions show), he constructs the first bourgeois interior in the English novel, heroically laying claim to a middle-class existence in (of all places) a cave. In the profoundest sense, all subsequent bourgeois dwellings are thus constructed; though more secure than Crusoe's, they too are subject to the vicissitudes of nature and history, and despite what their owners want to believe, they are not permanent. This may be one reason that Crusoe's enclosure is in a sense twice built—first in the novel's opening narration and a second time in Crusoe's journal, where many details are repeated. Readers never complain of the repetition because they enter so thoroughly into the bourgeois hero's paranoid fear that his home is not secure.

In describing the bourgeois interior of the nineteenth century, Walter Benjamin emphasizes the way furnishings retain the character of fortifications and reveal in their frequent use of diagonal arrangements "the unconscious retention of a posture of struggle and defense." The bourgeois of the nineteenth century burrows into his abode, secluding himself in his "cavern" just as Crusoe digs deeper and deeper into his cave, enlarging his living quarters "into several Apartments . . . one within another."[43] From the perspective of history, says Benjamin, it is as if the middle classes "will never quite have done with feudalism."[44] The eighteenth-century bourgeois adventurer's "castle" becomes the domestic fortress of the Victorian businessman. Defoe would establish for years to come the domestic interior as a medium, not simply for the bourgeois desire to reclaim an earlier, more stable middle state, and not simply for human inventiveness, but for both of these in the service of the bourgeois will to power.

Fanny's Room

Beginnings and Endings

Many writers who lived before Jane Austen, Defoe among them, register the rise of the spirit of capitalist enterprise in England, but Austen was the greatest novelist to have lived during the first stage of the Industrial Revolution. The England of her childhood was not wholly preindustrial, and the England of the last years of her life was not wholly industrialized, but contrasting the social contexts into which she was born and died may help us to understand some of the concrete particulars of the transition from agrarian to industrial society. With this transition came a new relation to the bourgeois home and its objects, one Austen witnessed at close hand and that she reinvents in her fiction with a less droll, more intellectual and pointed irony than that of Defoe. As we shall see, the domestic myth of *Robinson Crusoe* itself becomes a target of her irony in *Persuasion*.

Austen was born in 1775 in Steventon, a village of thirty-three families. Her father was a clergyman in a parish most of whose worshippers were tenant farmers, while her mother supervised her own poultry yard and cows. In this minuscule, homogenous, and unified society, the largest gathering Austen would have been likely to witness would number fifty or sixty at the small medieval church in Steventon on Sundays. Economy was home-centered, whether in the form of a cottage industry or farming. All depended on the seasons, such that the activity of everyone—high and low alike—was affected by seasonal changes. The servant who rose to light the fire early in the morning did so for himself as well as the Austens, and he would join in prayer each day with the family and the three or four boys who had come to live with the family for tutoring.

The village of Steventon was not on the beaten path to London but equidistant from two roads running there. The outer world was remote: news from the colonies reached Steventon several months after the event through rumors from naval ports, and travel was so slow in the 1770s that, like many other English towns, Steventon had its own time-system, four or five minutes behind the neighboring town.[1] The Austens were lower gentry in this isolated rural society. A neighboring squire, who might have served as the original for Fielding's Squire Western, once asked the educated Mr. Austen: "You know all about these sort of things. Do tell us. Is Paris in France, or France in Paris?"[2] Years later Austen would memorialize the small world of Steventon in *Emma,* whose heroine has never been to London or the seaside. The arrival of a new person from outside the village, like Frank Churchill, or an excursion beyond the community, like the expedition to Box Hill, is a momentous event in this novel.

In the words of the historian Peter Laslett, preindustrial society was one in which "everyone belonged to a group, a family group." Everything material was on a human scale, and "everything temporal was tied to the human life span too."[3] The death of a father could mean the end of a household business; marriage meant the creation of a new household. Work of all kinds depended on the weather, that troublesome secondary character in *Emma;* industry and agriculture lived in tandem.

Austen died in 1817 in Winchester, a city of thousands, where she had access to a weekly newspaper. To make way for commerce and the rising population, three old historic churches had been taken down; a hospital, debtor's prison, and new retail businesses related to the burgeoning tourist trade lined the streets.[4] The economy was dependent on the trade cycle rather than the seasons. The change in the scale of life from the world of her childhood, the increase in an anonymous population, the wider access to public affairs, the increasingly diversified economy, the decline in commonly held religious beliefs and habits—all had for at least a decade occupied Austen's attention. From 1801 to 1806 Austen had lived in Bath and subsequently made the contrast between the rural and the urban home central to the plot of *Mansfield Park.*

Austen never married, and this gave her an unusual vantage point from which to witness the shift from a society of families to a society of individuals. Few lived alone in the old society. As Laslett has shown, marriage meant entry into its full membership; as an unmarried woman, Austen never became part of the creation of a new household. Although unmarried and aged persons were not exiled from families to the extent they would be later in history, they were nonetheless peripheral to the families that supported them. Austen stood outside and behind her married contemporaries in this respect and was required to move to Chawton in 1809, after the death of her father, to a house provided by her brother. Her experience must have made her acutely aware of the transition out of a society in which the individual owed all or most aspects of his or her identity and livelihood to family and household. However imperfect the old society, it offered a measure of protection from social anonymity and anomie.

Austen moved to Winchester at the end of her life to be near her doctor, and her living circumstances there were similar to those of the impoverished, ill, and isolated Mrs. Smith in her last novel, *Persuasion.* Mrs. Smith inhabits rented rooms in an unfashionable section of Bath, and her room is her entire world. One of the last articulated domestic interiors in Austen's writing is that of Mrs. Smith: "Her accommodations were limited to a noisy parlour, and a dark bed-room behind, with no possibility of moving from one to the other without assistance."[5] Mrs. Smith's social isolation is not only a function of poor health but of circumstances that were becoming increasingly familiar: those of the urban individual living without strong connections to family or home.

The Rented Spaces of Persuasion

The transition from a society of houses (or families) to a society of rooms (or individuals) is most evident in the basic plot of *Persuasion* in which Sir Walter Elliott, as he slides from the life of a minor aristocrat to that of überbourgeois, moves from Kellynch Hall to rented lodgings in Bath. When his daughter Anne arrives in Bath, she is dismayed by her father's pleasure in his new dwelling: "she must sigh that her father should feel no degradation in his change; should see nothing to regret in the duties and dignity of the resident land-holder." She is again dismayed as her sister Elizabeth walks with "exultation from one drawing-room to the other, boasting of their space, at the possibility of that woman, who had been mistress of Kellynch Hall, finding extent to be proud of between two walls, perhaps thirty feet asunder."[6] The once powerful landed family now finds its importance in the grandeur of the domestic interior, whose objects are acquired through taste. The aristocratic family relics that the historian Lawrence Stone identifies as an intrinsic part of the inherited family seat—"deeds and patents of nobility, portraits of ancestors, family plate and jewels, and personal gifts from kings and queens"[7]—are not the source of status in Bath. Like many members of the nineteenth-century upper bourgeoisie and lower aristocracy, the Elliots no longer exercise their power directly on their estates but masquerade it in the style of their residences. Benjamin's use of the French word *étui* to describe the bourgeois interior now becomes clear in its more negative aspect, for the étui was used to refer to the sheath of a sword.[8]

The situation of Mr. Knightley in *Emma*—a novel that gives scant attention to domestic interiors—provides a useful contrast to that of Sir Walter. A resident landholder in Donwell parish all of his life, he possesses an undistinguished domestic interior—"rambling and irregular, with many comfortable and one or two handsome rooms"—but Austen follows the description of it with a revealing declaration: "It was just what it ought to be, and it looked what it was."[9] As hereditary landlord and magistrate, Mr. Knightley has no need for a pretentious interior to prove his authority because he is an authority in himself; his family has occupied Donwell Abbey for generations. The society of *Emma* is a society of houses; that of *Persuasion* is a society of rooms.

The shift from estate to real estate, as it were, also may be seen in the sheer number of rented spaces represented or referred to in *Persuasion,* a number that far exceeds that of any previous Austen work. Included are Kellynch Hall, Captain Harville's lodgings, the inn at Lyme, Sir Walter's rented rooms at Bath, Mrs. Smith's lodgings, and the other rented spaces occupied by the Musgroves, Harvilles, Dalrymples, and Lady Russell.[10] The dwellings of Mrs. Smith and the Elliots have already been mentioned—examples of impoverished gentility, on the one hand, and ostentatious wealth, on the other. In her sympathetic description of Captain Harville's lodgings at Lyme, however, Austen communicates the charm and vulnerability of a distinctly middle-class nineteenth-century interior. The Harvilles are an independent-spirited couple who know how "to turn the actual space to the best possible advantage," and their dwelling possesses something of the Dickensian feeling for home:

> On quitting the Cobb, they all went indoors with their new friends, and found rooms so small as none but those who invite from the heart could think capable of accommodating so many. Anne had a moment's astonishment on the subject herself; but it was soon lost in the pleasanter feelings which sprang from the sight of all the ingenious contrivances and nice arrangements of Captain Harville, to turn the actual space to the best possible advantage, to supply the deficiencies of lodging-house furniture,

and defend the windows and doors against the winter storms to be expected. The varieties in the fitting-up of the rooms, where the common necessaries provided by the owner, in the common indifferent plight, were contrasted with some few articles of a rare species of wood, excellently worked up, and with something curious and valuable from all the distant countries Captain Harville had visited, were more than amusing to Anne: connected as it all was with his profession, the fruit of its labours, the effect of its influence on his habits, the picture of repose and domestic happiness it presented made it to her a something more, or less, than gratification. . . . Captain Harville was no reader, but he had contrived excellent accommodations, and fashioned very pretty shelves, for a tolerable collection of well-bound volumes, the property of Captain Benwick. His lameness prevented him from taking much exercise; but a mind of usefulness and ingenuity seemed to furnish him with constant enjoyment within. He drew, he varnished, he carpentered, he glued; he made toys for the children, he fashioned new netting-needles and pins with improvements; and if everything else was done, sat down to his large fishing-net at one corner of the room.[11]

Harville's resourcefulness, industry, and inventiveness, even down to the building of shelves, bring to mind Robinson Crusoe, but the differences from Defoe's character point to a subtle critique of the adventurer. Unlike Crusoe, Harville does not claim ownership of his little spot on the planet, and the passage subtly acknowledges the transitory nature of all possession in the reference to "the winter storms to be expected." Even in this temporary dwelling, with an inhabitant who is no reader himself, a special place is fashioned for books or for a cultural past; the objects collected are not merely useful but beautiful; and Harville's activities consider the next generation ("he made toys for the children"). The entire passage pivots on a series of contrasts: small rooms vs. large hearts; deficiencies vs. contrivances; necessity vs. beauty; nearness vs. distance (common objects vs. those collected from afar); reading books vs. building bookshelves; disability vs. activity. Last but not least in this profound and playful dialectic, Austen presents us with a feminine image of a soldier who has fought honorably in a war. He is placed in a scene of "domestic happiness" as he sits down to sew his "large fishing-net," engaging in an activity normally associated with women.

In making the domestic interior a medium for human affection, ingenuity, and civilized value, Austen continues the tradition of the English "middle state." The Harvilles' interior indicates neither social ambition nor social decline but a via media of domestic moderation, contentment, and middle-class endurance. For all the contentment implied in this portrait, however, the dwelling's status as rental property makes the values it fosters transitory. The future that Austen imagines for her heroine suggests even greater uncertainty. When the novel's prepossessing egalitarian couple, Admiral and Mrs. Croft, defend the rightness of wives accompanying their Navy husbands on board ship—a domestic arrangement that the narrator clearly approves of for the heroine—we see Austen bidding an unsentimental farewell to the ideal of bourgeois domestic stability. If one considers the enormous value placed on the estate throughout Austen's fiction—the value of estates like Pemberley, which represent the dream of the bourgeoisie (and to some extent still do, if we are to judge from the lavish sets of television and film productions of the novel)—we may wonder at Austen's sudden indifference to bourgeois security. Unlike past heroines, Anne Elliot has no estate before her when she marries Captain Wentworth, and Austen places the accent on a questionable future by ending the novel shortly before the Battle of Waterloo. Although saddened to leave her ancestral home of Kellynch Hall early in the novel, Anne has no difficulty imagining domestic happiness in temporary lodgings. In other words, the *haute bourgeoisie* of *Persuasion* is no longer unequivocally identified with that symbol of cultural memory and stable economic value, the English estate. And the faith Austen appears to place in the Harvilles' haven of middle-class virtue is qualified in more ways than its rental status implies.

Like other rental spaces in *Persuasion,* the Harvilles' interior is conceived as closed to the outside, a private, isolated space whose connection to the exterior world is left undeveloped. The narrator allows for no transition from the Cobb to the Harville interior that might suggest a relation rather than a sharp separation between public and private: "On quitting the Cobb, they all went indoors," Austen tersely states. In contrast, the interiors and exteriors of earlier novels are mutually identified and the interiors often evoke the grounds. This is true even when the estates are riven by the rage for "improvement." Northanger Abbey has a modern wing built with no thought to "uniformity of architecture"[12]—that is, with no respect for the past or desire to integrate it into the present—but General Tilney is engaged in modernizing house and grounds alike. In *Pride and Prejudice,* Austen creates two estates to represent the historical tension implied in the drive to "improve": traditional Pemberley, which recalls Ben Jonson's Penshurst, and modern, ostentatious Rosings. Yet in portraits of both estates, inner and outer space is integrated. The grand rooms of Pemberley seem to flow out to nature—"from every window there were beauties to be seen"—and phrases that describe Pemberley's surrounding landscape are echoed in descriptions of the interior: the banks of the stream are "neither formal, nor falsely adorned" and the interior furniture is "neither gaudy nor uselessly fine." The rooms are as "lofty and handsome" as the grounds.[13]

In *Mansfield Park* Austen repeats the image of contrasting estates in her portraits of traditional Sotherton Manor and modern-built Mansfield. In the visit to Sotherton, the prospective bride's approach from afar and the admiring tour of the estate's impressive house and grounds parody Elizabeth's visit to Pemberley. Whereas Pemberley exists in harmonious relation to its past, at Sotherton long traditions have been abandoned, and the proprietor, Mr. Rushworth, is a buffoon whose inability to learn his part in the play is emblematic of his failure adequately to represent his estate, a symbol of cultural continuity secured in part through memory. The graceful integration of interior and exterior space at Pemberley is negatively reproduced in the way the "wilderness" at Sotherton, the godless exterior space that unleashes the seductive energies of Henry Crawford onto Maria Bertram, is matched by the vacated chapel within.

But in the portrait of Mansfield Park, something quite new to Austen occurs. There, Austen follows her investigation of the historical shift from traditional to modern society to its logical conclusion by representing in spatial terms the isolation of the individual that was the most profound consequence of this shift. In the modern-built Mansfield estate, all semblance of integration of interior and exterior, of equilibrium between private and public, breaks down. The rented rooms of *Persuasion,* as seemingly isolated from house or land as rooms on board ship would be, originate in Fanny Price's lonely room at Mansfield Park.

Fanny's Room

In *Mansfield Park* we encounter another bourgeois baronet, Sir Thomas Bertram. If the bourgeois character of Sir Walter Elliott is suggested in his sycophantic attitude toward the aristocracy, Sir Thomas's is established in his disapproval of it—he does not want his children to associate with the decadent, aristocratic friends of Mr. Yates—and in the way he conceives of himself as the Victorian paterfamilias of a family that extends into the lower middle class.[14] His identification with the interior space of his mansion is suggested in his stern rebuke to his children upon his return from Antigua, when he discovers that the physical space of his home has been violated by construction undertaken for the theatricals. Sir Thomas must leave Mansfield because it is not self-sustaining, and its dependence on the plantations in Antigua requires him to do what moralists like Addison had for centuries urged landowners not to do, live apart from their estates. When he departs, the already shaky moral foundation of his family begins to crumble.

What is at stake here is the equilibrium of the preindustrial home. As Austen knew from her own upbringing at Steventon, this equilibrium had not been maintained by denying either the public world or the world of intimate and sexual feeling, but by accepting their placement on the periphery of bourgeois experience, as it were, where they enriched without dominating the life of the bourgeois. At the center stood private property, which could not be greatly disturbed by these forces if a stable "middle state" was to be maintained. At Mansfield Park, however, the demands of public engagement are such that, as we have seen, Sir Thomas must leave the estate to attend to the holdings in Antigua. His absence looks forward to the separation of husband and home that would be a hallmark of industrial societies. When he departs and the theatricals take place, all of Mansfield is turned upside down by the illicit sexual energies released in performing the play. Even the servants at Mansfield are put out by the construction of the amateur theater.

In this full-scale treatment of the disruption of the ideal of preindustrial domestic life through forces within and without, Austen lays the groundwork for its ultimate dissolution in *Persuasion.* In that novel, a complete break with the domestic ideal of the old world occurs when the heroine of the novel rejects her ancestral home of Kellynch Hall, which she might have embraced (as Fanny ultimately embraces Mansfield) had she chosen to marry its heir, Sir William Elliott. It is almost as if Austen brings Sir William into the novel to clarify the rejection of this possibility. But the focus of *Mansfield Park* is very different. What appears to have engaged her at this stage with respect to the preindustrial domestic ideal is her class's desperate attachment to it as it was dissolving. This she explores through the character of her timid heroine, Fanny Price. By "attachment" I do not mean the defense of property and extension of capital within the gentry—the reasons for Sir Thomas's trip to Antigua—but the emotional, moral, and material attachment to a dying domestic ideal, a far more murky business. As we shall see, Austen's primary means of exploring the psychological and historical ambiguities of this attachment are the domestic interiors at Mansfield and Portsmouth.

Let us now turn to Fanny. In her capacity as dependent and guest at Mansfield, Fanny's status is not unlike that of the renters in *Persuasion*. She has no hereditary relation to the property, and her room within the mansion is isolated, deprived even of the warmth of a fire until well into the novel. Austen's first deep entrance into Fanny's subjective life occurs in chapter 16, when she offers an intricate description of Fanny's room. At night Fanny sleeps in the "little white attic," whereas in the daytime she makes use of the old school room—as if both a sleeping virgin and a vigilant one inhabit Mansfield Park in the person of Fanny, who is both acutely conscious yet unconscious of the insensitivity of those around her, perpetually receiving their insults while continuing to defer to and even idealize them. In the long passage from chapter 16 reproduced in the appendix to this work, Fanny retreats to the school room in the morning to decide if she should submit to the importunate demands of her cousins to act in the play: "[W]hat should she do? . . . The little white attic," where she had slept the night before, proves "incompetent to suggest any reply," but the old school room is more forthcoming. There, surrounded by her books, plants, furnishings (a transparency of Tintern Abbey, Julia's footstool), by treasured objects (her brother's childish sketch of his ship, Edmund's profile), and by all the gifts from the Bertram family, the agitated Fanny paces, thinks, and above all observes *things* in order to decide what she ought to do: "she could scarcely see an object in that room which had not an interesting remembrance connected with it."

To appreciate the uniqueness of this passage in the Austen oeuvre, we have only to think of the way Elizabeth Bennet's inner life is realized in the previous novel, *Pride and Prejudice*.

Whereas Elizabeth's consciousness unfolds as she reads and thinks over Darcy's letter, Fanny's is revealed spatially: her consciousness is inseparable from the things in her room. Austen creates a new world in this masterful scene, the world of Fanny's circumambient self. It is here that the narrative suddenly thickens, one-third of the way through the novel and at the beginning of Fanny's maturity. Just as the most stable moral consciousness in the novel belongs to Fanny, the only secure moral space is her room, in spite or because of the fact that the room vibrates with her uncertainty. Here the domestic interior becomes the medium for Fanny's consciousness, indeed for consciousness itself, since Fanny is the only fully aware character in a society of the morally obtuse. Even Edmund deludes himself in the scene that follows the schoolroom passage, when he rationalizes his submission to the urgings of his siblings to perform in the play.

The East room has a prehistory, as it were; it was the schoolroom of Fanny and her cousins, and although it has become "useless" to others in the house, it continues to be a place of education and contemplation for Fanny. In containing within it an image of the ancient ruin of Tintern Abbey, the room reaches back into the nation's history, alluding as well to the recently published poem by Wordsworth, "Lines Composed Five Miles above Tintern Abbey," in which the relations between time and space, past and present, are also meditated within an individual consciousness. But whereas in Wordsworth's poem, the medium through which contemplation is conveyed is nature, in Austen's novel, it is the domestic interior.

Fanny revives the history and extends the vista of the room through the objects she has collected, including the "transparencies"—an image of memory itself, since she sees through these objects into the past. The initial dialectical tension revealed in the passage, then, is that between past and present, but this opposition is introduced by another, more psychological one—that between waking and sleeping or consciousness and unconsciousness—which saturates the entire scene. Fanny's struggle to "find her way to her duty" is conceived of as a struggle to see clearly: to discover "her way" through observing the things around her. Again, the difference from Elizabeth Bennet's crisis is striking, for Elizabeth's struggle takes place while she is contemplating words, whereas Fanny's is a matter of physical observation.

The process of discovery, of unfolding consciousness, is understood in terms of the things with which Fanny is able to communicate. Unlike the mute little attic, which cannot answer the question of what she ought to do, the East room speaks through objects: "Every thing was a friend, or bore her thoughts to a friend." Her brother's sketch, Edmund's profile, the geraniums, the presents she has received from her cousins: each has something to tell her. As she struggles inwardly, she looks outward, seeking "strength," "counsel," and "air," even life itself, from the objects around her, attempting "to see if by looking at Edmund's profile she could catch any of his counsel, or by giving air to her geraniums she might inhale a breeze of mental strength herself."

Many of the memory-filled objects Fanny has collected around her are bought objects, acquired either through money given to her or money spent on her. She collected plants and books, Austen makes clear, only after she had money at her disposal. As Fanny gazes upon the gifts from her cousins, "she grew bewildered as to the amount of debt which all these kind remembrances produced." What Fanny owes to herself morally—"to find her way to her duty"—is here threatened by what she owes to others. Fanny's dilemma returns us to the question of use: how *useful* is the East room to Fanny if its guilt-producing objects prevent her from doing her duty? The primary purpose of the East room, which had always been to provide consolation, is destroyed by what nourishes it, for the objects that reassure her also unnerve her. When the scene is interrupted by Edmund's tapping, Fanny is at an impasse, "bewildered" by the debt that the gifts have produced and unable to determine where her obligations lie. As her meditation focuses on material debt, Fanny's judgment founders. At the center of this impasse is the ambivalent nature of things themselves, their dual capacity as historical-economical objects and as repositories of memory.

Fanny's impasse is reflected in the dialectical tension that pervades the passage—a tension between ideas of sleeping and waking, uselessness and usefulness, consolation and doubt, past and present, tears and affection, affliction and charm, and, most of all, between objects as signs of financial dependency on the one hand, and objects as embodiments of affection on the other. As she tries to *see her way out* of the forest of objects that represents her dilemma, "the table between the windows" is covered by objects of "remembrance" that tell of "the amount of debt." Located *between* the windows, these objects do not obstruct the view, but to look out, to see the world, as it were, one must look away from them. One must deny both the material-economic reality the objects represent and the affectionate memories they evoke. What then would remain for Fanny? It is by means of such details that her "morally impossible" situation—a phrase used in the first chapter by Mrs. Norris—is exposed.

The hierarchy of *things* in the passage moves from collected objects (plants and books) to objects cast off by other members of the family and treasured by Fanny (transparencies, Julia's footstool, family profiles) to given objects, beginning with her brother's sketch and ending with "present upon present" from her cousins. On a descending scale, the highest value is placed on the conscious choice reflected in collected objects, the lowest on objects bestowed by those with too much to give, whose gifts are actually a form of trash, as the allusion to objects "thought unworthy of being anywhere else" suggests. Jane Austen, not Fanny, constructs this hierarchy, for Fanny is too immersed in the world of the East room to make these distinctions. With affliction and affection "now so blended together," Fanny cannot extricate herself from the *debt* without violating the *duty* that she proposes to perform. For her, as I have suggested, both debt and duty merge irrevocably in the objects themselves.

When she later rejects the marriage proposal of Henry Crawford and greatly offends Sir Thomas in doing so, our proto-Victorian heroine shows that she is now fully capable of distinguishing material debt from moral duty, and the novel appears to turn away from the dialectical consciousness explored in chapter 16 to a unilateral affirmation of individualist morality. In spite of the sense of shame she feels before her benefactor, Fanny is glad to be sent home to her natural family, to a place that she assumes will nurture her in the individualism that has so offended Sir Thomas. But Portsmouth fails her, and *Mansfield Park* resolves its famously ambiguous plot without sacrificing a fraction of what might be called its dialectical intractability.

Portsmouth and Nostalgia for the Rural Past

What happens in Portsmouth? At her family's home, Fanny is surprised to discover what Austen has already made clear in chapter 16: Fanny's terrible dependency on things, both in their material aspect, for the comfort they provide, and in their emotional importance as embodiments of memory. Traveling to Portsmouth, Fanny is convinced that the pleasure of being with her family will make amends for their relative poverty: luxury and "manner Fanny did not want. Would they but love her, she should be satisfied."[15] Taking for granted domestic surroundings as peaceful and amenable as those of Mansfield, she assumes that now that the younger Prices are grown up, "there would be leisure and inclination for every comfort" and that she and her mother "would soon be what mother and daughter ought to be to each other."[16] What she experiences, however, nearly debilitates her: "Fanny was almost stunned. The smallness of the house, and thinness of the walls, brought everything so close to her, that, added to the fatigue of her journey . . . she hardly knew how to bear it."[17] Separated from the familiar things on which her very consciousness depends, Fanny can barely function.

Austen uses the urban context of Portsmouth to explore bourgeois attachment to its rural past. In Fanny's craven longing for Mansfield, she repeatedly compares the tumult and confinement, the "bad air [and] bad smells," of the city to the pleasures of life in the country:

> It was sad to Fanny to lose all the pleasures of spring. She had not known before what pleasures she *had* to lose in passing March and April in a town. . . . To be losing such pleasures was no trifle; to be losing them, because she was in the midst of closeness and noise, to have confinement, bad air, bad smells, substituted for liberty, freshness, fragrance, and verdure, was infinitely worse.[18]

> [The] sun's rays falling strongly into the parlor, instead of cheering, made her still more melancholy; for sun-shine appeared to her a totally different thing in a town and in the country. Here, its power was only a glare, stifling, sickly glare, serving but to bring forward stains and dirt that might otherwise have slept. There was neither health nor gaiety in sun-shine in a town. She sat in a blaze of oppressive heat, in a cloud of moving dust.[19]

The quiet and comforting routines of spacious, unpolluted Mansfield are now idealized in her memory: "At Mansfield . . . no abrupt bursts, no tread of violence was ever heard; all proceeded in a regular course of cheerful orderliness." The reader may find it difficult to recall the cheerfulness of Mansfield, but Fanny is blinded by her misery, and even her aunt's cruelties— "the little irritations, sometimes introduced by aunt Norris"— become "trifling" in comparison to the "ceaseless tumult of her present abode."[20] The luxury and "manner" that she had been confident she could do without have now become necessary to her. Fanny clings to her memory of the property itself, to its material comfort and security, and to the natural beauties denied her in a city. Her longing for Mansfield, even to the point where she deceives herself about the "trifling" injuries she endured there, is understandable not simply because of the attractions of material comfort but because of the capacity of memory to be shaped by the circumstances one is in, the subject of recent research on memory by Daniel L. Schacter. Fanny's nostalgia for Mansfield is conditioned by her urban circumstances—"she had not known before what pleasures she *had* to lose"—and may be seen as emblematic of an entire generation's nostalgia for rural life as it settled in the city.

Manifestations of this nostalgia survive today in the form of a fantasy that Austen knew well: the dream of the rural cottage. It is to a "cottage" that Fanny and her brother plan to escape from the world later in life, and in a "cottage" that the superrich Robert Ferrars envisions a more simpering retreat from London social life in *Sense and Sensibility*. In the late eighteenth century, bourgeois desire for a second home or retreat appears in the fashion for *cottages ornées*, those gussied-up rural dwellings that anticipate sentimentalized images of home on sale in shopping malls across America. Inspired by longing for the preindustrial past, these contemporary images often reveal their fantasy-driven character in horticultural contradictions. In Thomas Kinkade's widely reprinted *Evening at Swanbrooke, Thomashire*, for example, all four seasons compete for attention at once.[21] The trees in the background exhibit the red and gold of fall foliage, yet snow dusts the roof and path, suggesting winter. A stream is rushing in the foreground with spring run-off, and what appear to be azaleas, bowers of roses, delphiniums, and hollyhocks are in bloom, though each is known to bloom in a different cycle from May to August. A similar disregard for the realities of rural landscape is reflected in Henry Crawford's plans for renovating the parsonage at Thornton Lacey in *Mansfield Park:* "The farm-yard must be cleared away entirely," he advises, "and planted to shut out the blacksmith's shop."[22] All signs of the living, working rural community are to be effaced in pursuit of the bourgeois fantasy of rural life.

In *The Victorian Parlour,* Thad Logan writes of the enormous popularity of scenes depicting cottage interiors in nineteenth-century paintings, speculating that these idealized cottages served "to reassure a Victorian audience that financial success was not necessary to domestic happiness."[23] But they may also have reassured bourgeois viewers of what financial success could provide: even more security. The Victorian bourgeois desire for a secondary domestic space takes us back to Crusoe's "bower," from which he is able to gaze back on his primary residence or "fortress" and contemplate his security. In other words, the second home, cottage, or "bower" promises the *feeling* of peaceful security that the primary residence (in spite or because of the measures taken to secure it) fails to provide. Like Fanny when she returns to her native Portsmouth, the bourgeois feels homesick even when she is at home.

Pernicious Property

The description of Fanny's emotional identification with the objects in her room in chapter 16 prefigures this homesickness for the estate as a whole as it appears in her imagination at Portsmouth. Placed between Fanny's isolation from Mansfield in chapter 16 and her marriage to Mansfield at the end of the novel (which is how the union with Edmund is conceived), the experience of Portsmouth is used to develop the larger, more disturbing implications of the new relation to objects that came with the demise of the old society. In the Portsmouth chapters, bourgeois identification with property is represented in profoundly negative form. Natural family relations are proven powerless before the security and comfort that wealth provides. The attachment of Fanny's own mother appears to be minimal after the long separation; affectionate to her daughter on the day of her arrival, she proceeds to forget about Fanny afterward: "The instinct of nature was soon satisfied, and Mrs

Price's attachment had no other source."[24] What might the other sources of family attachment be? Those of home and community in traditional society, strengthened over time and nourished by a sense of place. When one is deprived of a common past in a given community, "the ties of blood," Fanny discovers, are "little more than nothing."[25] As Ruth Perry writes in *Novel Relations,* "In *Mansfield Park,* Jane Austen stages Fanny Price's return to Portsmouth to dramatize the dissolution of her ties with her family of origin."[26] Perry argues that "the earlier moral system that honored kin obligations" was being radically undermined by the forces of capitalism, a change that helps to account for the "increasing complication of the laws concerning property and inheritance and women's diminished right to family property."[27] In the new, urban circumstances of Portsmouth, property ownership and inheritance take on disturbing characteristics—raw and infantile—in the following minor episode.

Fanny's two sisters, Susan and Betsey, get into a squabble about the possession of a silver knife that Susan claims their dead sister Mary left to her upon her deathbed. The mother favors the younger child, however, and Betsey is allowed to play with the knife, a strange object for a mother to permit as a toy. The object is invested with heartrending associations for Fanny because the dying child, whom she loved, treasured it in the last weeks of her life, and the coarse bickering that Fanny must endure over it is one of the most trying episodes in her visit at Portsmouth: "Every feeling of duty, honour, and tenderness was wounded" by it.[28] Both the pettiness of bourgeois attachment to things and the ineradicably human, affective nature of the bond that things inspire in us are exposed in this episode: it is a knife, an object that harms, not a spoon, an object that feeds, that is disputed.

At the end of *Mansfield Park,* Mansfield is purged of the pernicious influence of Mrs. Norris, and Maria Bertram is banished. These events are like the excisions of a knife, and they are brought about through Fanny, whose honorable refusal to marry Henry Crawford initiates the actions that result in them. With profound ambivalence, Austen allows that Fanny's attachment to the place that humbled her leads to her ascendancy in the bourgeois household, and the cruel class morality that brought Fanny to Mansfield in the first place is finally validated. In the Edenic description of Mansfield Park upon Fanny's return from Portsmouth, the freshness, growth, and anticipation of early summer—"that delightful state, when farther beauty is known to be at hand"[29]—is set off against the illness, melancholy, and deprivations of the interior. In this insidious contrast, which looks forward to Dickens's description of the Maylies' rural residence in *Oliver Twist,* both the growth and the decay of the Victorian bourgeoisie are ominously prefigured.

Charles Dickens and
the Victorian Addiction
to Dwelling

The Bourgeois Domestic Ideal and Dickens's Life

A dialectic of growth and decay is rooted in bourgeois history.[1] The Industrial Revolution, which entered its first stage in the late eighteenth century, granted the bourgeois class unprecedented power at the same time that it steadily eroded bourgeois domestic traditions that had been in place for centuries. The sense of enclosure, the comfortable distance from a public world, the equilibrium within the privacy of the agrarian home, in which activities and rituals were tied to the natural cycle: all were disrupted by industrialization. In the portrait of Fanny Price at Portsmouth, Austen shows the homesick response to this upheaval; and in her description of the Prices' townhouse, in which home and street are brought into close proximity, she looks forward to the urban dwellings one finds in every Dickens novel. The bourgeois now lived in a world where privacy had to be created.

The interpenetration of private and public spaces and the "dangerous contiguousness" of the domestic and the criminal spheres are a primary means of registering the social anxieties created by the industrial city in Dickens's works. As Gareth Cordery suggests, there is no need for Bill Sykes to take Oliver Twist out of the middle-class domestic world of the Maylie cottage and back to Fagin's den "because his bourgeois fears and anxieties do that for him, and in doing so mock the middle class attempt to wall him in."[2] Cruikshank's illustration of Oliver sleeping at Rose Maylie's cottage, as Fagin and Monks stand at the open lattice watching him, suggests that the violation of bourgeois space is both reality and dream, both something that was happening and something that was feared (p. 63). Here the social and psychological readings of bourgeois dwelling overlap, and we are once again reminded of Benjamin's use of Freud to interpret the nineteenth-century resistance to urban "shock." Like the vulnerability of consciousness to traumatic memory, the protective cover of bourgeois domesticity is never entirely secure.

In the image of the sleeping Oliver, the sense of invaded privacy is communicated by means of the central placement of the window. (In Dutch genre paintings of interiors, a feeling of protected enclosure is achieved in part by placing windows to the side of the frame. Often, as in Vermeer's *The Love Letter,* light comes from an unseen window, intensifying the sense of privacy.) The trespassers, who wear menacing expressions, are placed directly before us and make us anxious for Oliver's safety. Dickens worked closely with Cruikshank on the details in the illustrations, and his ambivalence about the threat posed by Fagin is suggested in the position of the vase. It would almost appear that Fagin is bringing Oliver flowers in one hand and holding a dagger (in actuality, his cane) in the other.

In directing Cruikshank to create illustrations such as this one, Dickens exploits the fact that rich and poor sections of urban areas were in close proximity, a fact that the bourgeoisie successfully denied, in part through creating unusually cosseted interior spaces. In his narrative descriptions of the domestic interior, snug spaces abound, and repeated references to walls, closets, corners, and drawers suggest a longing for protection and security. Like David Copperfield, who delights in the snug bed within a closet within his mother's room or the tiny bed he occupies at the Peggottys, Dickens himself was drawn to the coziness of the smaller space within the larger. He erected a chalet in the garden of Gad's Hill that resembled a doll's house and enjoyed staying in snug quarters abroad.[3] The storage of objects at the Midshipman's in *Dombey and Son,* in which "objects of brass and glass" find their home in "mahogany nests," cases, corners, and cushions, gives the impression that "extraordinary precautions" are being taken to ensure stability.[4] The fortresslike character of the Victorian domestic interior inspired Walter Benjamin to write that the "nineteenth century, like no other century, was addicted to dwelling. It conceived the residence as the receptacle for the person, and it encased him with all his appurtenances so deeply in the dwelling's interior that one might be reminded of a compass case, where the instrument with all its accessories lies embedded in deep, usually violet folds of velvet. What didn't the nineteenth century invent some sort of casing for!"[5] By creating an atmosphere of airless enclosure, the Victorian interior, with its dense layers of drapery and heavy furniture, both conceals and reveals the longing for the more static environment of the past. The image of a compass embedded in folds of velvet further suggests, as Diana Fuss points out, "that the modern subject, surrounded by expensive commodities, has lost its bearings."[6]

In spite or perhaps because of these anxieties, the bourgeois domestic ideal thrived in the public imagination, and no artist was more passionately attached to it than Dickens.[7] In the words of G. K. Chesterton, "Dickens did not write what the people wanted. Dickens wanted what the people wanted."[8] No one sought to bring the bourgeois ideal into relation with modern society more earnestly than he. This might not have been the case but for the definitive event of Dickens's childhood. In 1824 the Dickens family experienced in microcosm the destruction of bourgeois security, at a time when the bourgeoisie as a whole was experiencing the great impact of industrialization.

The story is well known. Under the threat of imprisonment for debt, Dickens's father took his twelve-year-old son out of school and sent him to work at a shoe-blacking factory. Soon after, John Dickens and the rest of the family entered debtor's prison, where they remained for about three months. After a windfall inheritance led to his release and bourgeois family life

"Monks and the Jew," George Cruikshank, from *Oliver Twist* (1837–39)

resumed, young Dickens was reluctantly received back into the home—his mother was in favor of his remaining at the factory—and then sent to school, but he never told anyone of the experience at Warrens Blacking factory, not his friends at school and not even his wife and children years later. Long after he had established himself as a writer, he allowed his friend and biographer, John Forster, to read a narrative of the experience that has since become known as the Autobiographical Fragment. Together with the different renderings of bourgeois domesticity in the fiction, the Fragment suggests that the experience of being cast out of the bourgeoisie, then reluctantly permitted to reenter it, was decisive in shaping Dickens's vision of bourgeois existence as a whole and of domestic space in particular. For Dickens, the domestic interior became the site of both inordinate joy and anxiety.

To be banished from home, from the *heimlich,* and from all that he loved, made Dickens's return—especially to a mother who did not seem to want him—disturbing in the extreme. In the Fragment, he writes of returning home with "a relief so strange that it was like oppression." The degree to which he felt himself unworthy is implied in the well-known confession: "I never afterwards forgot, I never shall forget, I never can forget, that mother was warm for my being sent back," he writes.[9] The curious uneasiness underlying the bourgeois domestic ideal throughout the oeuvre may go back to this early experience, to the young Dickens's tentative return to his bourgeois family. In Cruikshank's illustration "Oliver at Mrs. Maylie's Door," the abject Oliver is greeted by ferocious dogs as he begs for bourgeois protection, while towering adults glare at him as if he were street vermin (opposite). The inhabitants of the respectable household appear far more threatening than the criminals in the earlier illustration.

From the early novels on, moments of entry into bourgeois households are charged with complex and contradictory emotions. Even Pickwick's arrival at Manor Farm, Dingley Dell, the most idealized of all of Dickens's domestic locations, is fraught with difficulty. Arriving at long last on a recalcitrant horse, Pickwick is tired and filthy: "torn clothes, lacerated faces, dusty shoes, exhausted looks" must be transformed before he is admitted to the parlor, symbol of bourgeois respectability.[10] Like David Copperfield entering Dover, Pickwick must be cleansed before he is permitted to enter the bourgeois circle and given food.

Dingley Dell is a place of playfulness, repose, and abundance, comically symbolized by that "natural curiosity," the Fat Boy, the mischievous child who is always hungry, yet always seemingly sated and falling asleep.[11] With its fire blazing in

"Oliver at Mrs. Maylie's Door," George Cruikshank, from
Oliver Twist (1837–39)

the kitchen, it is the incandescent center of community, a middle-class Victorian version of Pemberley; yet halfway through
Pickwick Papers it recedes and the opposite pole of Dickens's
imagination assumes control as Pickwick approaches the Fleet.
The Fleet is everything that Dingley Dell is not—a place of
sleeplessness, violence, and scarcity—and the geographical distance between the two settings expresses the disjunction between the bourgeois domestic ideal and modern society itself.

Throughout his career, Dickens worked to overcome this
disjunction and bring the two poles of his imagination together. The years most critical to this effort are those leading

up to the publication of his autobiographical novel, *David Cop-perfield.* In these years, roughly from 1847 to 1850, Dickens's struggle to realize the bourgeois domestic ideal, both in his personal life and in his fiction, seems to have been most vigorous. These are the years in which his marriage to Catherine Hogarth began to decline, a decline that Dickens, bourgeois husband and father par excellence, fought against with an uncomprehending, despairing determination. Dickens himself was addicted to dwelling, one may say, and in many ways he sought to extricate himself from the bourgeois domestic haven he had created. In 1848, in a letter to Mary Cowden Clarke, he writes: "I loathe domestic hearths. I yearn to be a Vagabond . . . Why have I seven children . . . taken on for an indefinite time at vast expense?"[12] Yet in 1856, Dickens made the massive purchase of Gad's Hill Place, realizing at last the dream of his childhood, which was to occupy the mansion that his father had told him long before could be his one day if he worked hard.

The period leading up to the publication of *David Copperfield* also witnessed Dickens's efforts to establish, with the philanthropist Angela Burdett Coutts, Urania Cottage, a middle-class domestic "home" where prostitutes released from prison could reform their characters. The Urania Cottage project, which eventually failed, represents Dickens's effort to bring about a kind of shotgun wedding between the domestic ideal and modern society. In the letters between Burdett Coutts and Dickens, the project is often referred to as the "Asylum" or the "Home," typical names for social welfare institutions, but it eventually took the name of "cottage," the mythic locus of bourgeois domestic happiness in so many Dickens novels.

In his letter to the prostitutes who might enter Urania Cottage, Dickens sings its praises: "In this home, which stands in a pleasant country lane and where each may have her little flower-garden if she pleases, [those who enter] will be treated with the greatest kindness: will lead an active, cheerful healthy life: will learn many things it is profitable and good to know, and being entirely removed from all who have any knowledge of their past career will begin life afresh and be able to win a good name and character."[13] The eventual "new life," however, would not be in England but Australia, where they would be sent for marriage. Meanwhile, they would be improved "by education and example" and rendered "an innocently cheerful Family, while they live there."

Dickens places great emphasis on the rule of secrecy in his letters to Burdett Coutts: the women's "past lives should never be referred to at the Home," not communicated among the inmates, and revealed by superintendents and matrons on pain of dismissal.[14] Inhabiting a suspended state in which the past was not acknowledged and the future in Australia scarcely imaginable, the women of Urania Cottage often failed to rise in the moral marking system designed to evaluate their behavior. Roughly half of the fifty-six women admitted by 1853 left of their own accord, were expelled for misconduct, ran away, or returned to prostitution on the passage to Australia.[15] In a final note of irony, Dickens himself had to withdraw from engagement with the home in 1858 because no respectable husband separated from his wife could continue a partnership with an unmarried woman of Burdett Coutts's social standing.

The parallels between Urania Cottage and Dickens's representation of David Copperfield's life at Dover (where, like the prostitutes, he is to "do over" his life) may tell us something about the way he imagined his own degradation and rescue from Warrens Blacking. Like the prostitutes whose pasts are never spoken of—and like Dickens himself, who told no one at Wellington House Academy of the factory experience—David Copperfield keeps the secret of his past when he attends Dr. Strong's academy. And like the women at Urania Cottage, who are placed on trial before "their good conduct and self-denial" earn them entrance into the "Society" of the home,[16] David must prove himself to his aunt before he is allowed to reenter bourgeois life and attend school. The rules the inmates would live by are the same rules as those of Dr. Strong's academy in

David Copperfield, and just as David is given new clothes to symbolize a new identity, each inmate is issued a uniform at Urania Cottage.[17] (Dickens stressed the symbolic importance of the color to Burdett Coutts.) The essential ingredients of the domestic idyll longed for by David Copperfield and epitomized in Dickens's Christmas books—domestic order, cleanliness, and efficiency—were put in place at Urania Cottage.[18]

The prostitutes were sure to feel, wrote Dickens, "the power of beginning life anew,"[19] a power that the young Dickens may have felt when he was taken out of the factory and returned to school, and that he recreates for David Copperfield. Yet for twelve-year-old Dickens, beginning life anew did not of course mean what it must have meant to the prostitutes at Urania Cottage. To him, it was a question of being welcomed home. As the Fragment makes clear, it occurred to Dickens in his maturity that he was entitled to something more than the cold reception he received from his mother. He was entitled to be welcomed home, entitled to be loved. Though he had occupied a degraded social position, it was not his fault. He was deserving of a son's position, a son's inheritance. In short, the pervasive psychology of David Copperfield replicates this state of mind: the passionate wish for, *demand* for, entitlement. *These pages must show* that I am *the hero of my own life.* In *David Copperfield,* bourgeois man affirms himself. At the end of the novel, David is pictured in middle age, happy, successful, and entitled to be so, because he is the hero of his own life.

Because of the style of the immensely popular *David Copperfield,* its consummate achievement of sincerity of tone, Dickens's devoted contemporary audience did not of course question the novel's opening proposition, or consider that a man who at middle age considers himself the hero of his own life would in all likelihood be insufferable. If we add to this preening self-image certain facts of David's life—such as those featured in illustrations that haunt the narrative like guilty memories: his indirect responsibility for the firing of Mr. Mell and the tragedy of Little Emily's seduction (David introduces his friend

Steerforth into her family circle)—Dickens's success in getting his readers to like David is all the more striking. Most ingenious of all is the moral evasion accomplished in the blacking factory episode (long ago noted by George Bernard Shaw and George Orwell) in which the reader is permitted to feel that there is nothing wrong with the other children working in the factory; it is a sin only where David is concerned, because he is a gentleman's son being "put to work not fit for [him]."[20]

When David enters the middle-class world of Dover and of Dr. Strong's academy, he does what the prostitutes of Urania Cottage were required to do upon entrance into the respectable "Society" of the home and what Dickens's paradigmatic bourgeois, Podsnap, does in *Our Mutual Friend:* he denies the existence of any other world, any world different from the hermetically sealed environment of the bourgeoisie. Dickens places emphasis on David's knowledge: "But, troubled as I was by my want of boyish skill [at Dr. Strong's], and of book-learning too, I was made infinitely more uncomfortable by the consideration, that, in what I did know, I was much farther removed from my companions than in what I did not." His mind runs on *what people would think* if they knew he was acquainted with King's Bench Prison, for example, or if they were made aware of "how knowing [he] was (and was ashamed to be)" of London street life.[21] So strong is David's sense of the shameful difference between his past self and the self he must become that he accomplishes an absolute dissociation within himself: "That little fellow seems to be no part of me; I remember him as something left behind me upon the road of life—as something I have passed, rather than have actually been—and almost think of him as of some one else."[22] Entrance into the coveted space of the bourgeoisie is here imagined as a profound self-effacement. In a passage from *David Copperfield* that will be considered at the end of this chapter, David pictures himself stationed for the first time in Aunt Betsey's interior as a "dusty self" set amid luminous domestic objects, as if he were himself decaying faster than the objects around him.

In *Great Expectations,* the pursuit of genteel status results in a similar self-estrangement in Pip, but one that Dickens examines with a more conscious critical spirit. David's desperate flight from London, undertaken to reenter the bourgeoisie, lands him in the interior of his aunt's cottage, where he is grateful to be locked in his room at night, but Pip is summoned to Satis House by Miss Havisham and escorted there unwillingly by Pumblechook, as if he were a criminal: "I was then delivered over to Mr Pumblechook, who formally received me as if he were Sheriff." Whereas David's ritual cleansing gives him pleasure—"The bath was a great comfort," he croons—Pip's ablutions are a form of violence: he is "soaped, and kneaded, and toweled, and thumped, and harrowed, and rasped," while "the ridgy effect of a wedding-ring" is passed "unsympathetically" over his countenance.[23] Entering the bourgeois interior is always an ordeal for Dickens's protagonists, but in *Great Expectations* it marks entrance into a kind of torture chamber of adult sexual sanction.

Like Mrs. Clennam's house in *Little Dorrit,* Satis House is paradigmatic of the bourgeois interior as fortress, prison, and tomb. The house is protected by an iron gate, its windows either walled up or barred. Because the "great front entrance had two chains across it," Estella admits Pip through a side door.[24] They enter a dark passage and find their way to Miss Havisham, who, like a witch in a fairy tale, seems to have cast a spell on the house. Everything is at a standstill, as if turned to stone. Miss Havisham herself, with her "shroud of a dress," is an image of death itself.[25] Her old "bride-cake," now infested with spiders and mice, sits on the long table on which she herself will be laid when she dies: the mummified, maternal body. "Now you all know where to take your stations," she cries to her relatives, the Pockets, as she pounds the table with her stick, "when you come to feast upon me."[26]

A wide variety of novelistic and cinematic dwellings coming after the portrait of Satis House (and the gothic fictions that influenced it) owe to Dickens their equation of the bourgeois interior with neurosis. In George Cukor's *Gaslight* (1944), the instability of the heroine, memorably played by Ingrid Bergman, is confirmed long before her mental disorientation takes place by the mere fact of her ghoulish hereditary residence. As Howard Eiland writes:

> *Gaslight* is all about the Victorian domestic interior—about infinite degrees of light and shadow, manifold concealment, the most intricate disposition of space in a drawing room, about locked drawers, curtains, handbags, pockets, every sort of cover and recess. House as fortress, prison, and ruin—the film is equivalent of Satis House. Full of ghosts. Such a place is inevitably the scene of a crime, its traces everywhere obscured by the insidious fog, the equivocal gaslight. Circuitously, pausing at every untoward station, magnetized by the profusion of objects, we enter the madness of the Victorian interior.[27]

Dating from the nineteenth century, mental institutions were often called "private mental homes" and, like prisons, drew on the styles of Victorian domestic architecture, suggesting perhaps an unconscious cultural recognition of the bourgeois household as asylum.

All of these associations must be set aside to appreciate the originality of Satis House and the critique of normalcy that it embodies. Pip enters the house at the onset of puberty—he is smaller than Estella, who is his same age, because girls mature more quickly—and the social-sexual education he receives there is an education in repression. Like the seeds housed in Pumblechook's dark drawers, Pip will not bloom naturally but will have his natural impulses diverted by the perverse sexual part Estella forces him to play. Much like Dickens's first love, Maria Beadnell, who persecuted Dickens with her unrelenting coquettishness, Estella uses sex and class together to humiliate Pip. The adolescent boy's vulnerability before feminine prerogative is matched by its reverse in Miss Havisham's adult vulnerability before the masculine license of Compeyson, the man who deserted her.

The interior of Satis House is a grim parody of the standard Victorian interior in which the bourgeois owners leave traces of themselves on their possessions, a phenomenon that Benjamin identifies as peculiar to the nineteenth-century interior: "If you enter a bourgeois room of the 1880s, for all the coziness it radiates, the strongest impression you will receive may well be, 'You've got no business here.' And in fact you have no business in that room, for there is no spot on which the owner has not left his mark—the ornaments on the mantelpiece, the antimacassars on the armchairs, the transparencies in the windows, the screen in front of the fire."[28] In "The Interior, The Trace," Benjamin alludes to the widespread use of "plush" in nineteenth-century interiors, the velvet material in which "traces are left especially easily."[29] The bourgeois seeks to compensate for the absence of any trace of his private life in the world outside the home. Miss Havisham's room is full of remnants of her younger self: her wedding dress, shoe, veil, jewels, watch and chain, gloves, flowers, and prayer book are "heaped about the looking-glass," the instrument of self-reflection. Satis House literalizes Benjamin's formula for the interior, which is to feel sick for home even while one is there. Miss Havisham languishes for her former self, just as the house itself seems to sicken for its former glory.

Pip's task is to recognize all of this:

> It was not in the first few moments that I saw all these things, though I saw more of them in the first moments than might be supposed. But, I saw that everything within my view which ought to be white, had been white long ago, and had lost its lustre, and was faded and yellow. I saw that the bride within the bridal dress had withered like the dress, and like the flowers, and had no brightness left but the brightness of her sunken eyes. I

saw that the dress had been put upon the rounded figure of a young woman, and that the figure upon which
it now hung loose, had shrunk to skin and bone. Once, I
had been taken to see some ghastly waxwork at the Fair,
representing I know not what impossible personage lying
in state. Once, I had been taken to one of our old marsh
churches to see a skeleton in the ashes of a rich dress, that
had been dug out of a vault under the church pavement.
Now, waxwork and skeleton seemed to have dark eyes
that moved and looked at me. I should have cried out, if I
could.[30]

In *David Copperfield,* Dickens uses an arresting metaphor for
the experience of recollection, one that applies to the passage quoted before: the metaphor of a "shining transparency"
through which David sees his "earlier life moving along."[31] The
past is superimposed on the present, as on a transparency. Different levels of time interpenetrate one another as Pip, seeking
to determine his precise degree of consciousness at the moment
he first laid eyes on Miss Havisham, revaluates what he once
saw. Now an adult, he raises to the level of cognition everything he took in at the time, both what he saw and imagined
he saw, closing the gap between past and present like the con-
tracting coils of a spiral. Full of contradiction (luster/dullness;
roundness/emaciation; life/death), his observations induce ver-
tigo as they teach him that to preserve the past is to commit
oneself to decay. White changes to yellow, luster to dullness,
roundness to emaciation, and finally, life to death as the repetitive cadences of the sentences usher us into the vault with the
"skeleton in the ashes of a rich dress." Like the interiors Benjamin describes in *The Arcades Project,* the interior of Satis house
"is a stimulus to intoxication and dream."[32] Miss Havisham
herself is intoxicated with the past—the estate once housed a
brewery—and Pip has visions as he walks on the casks in the
rank garden.

In this reading of what is arguably the richest imaginative

space in all of Victorian fiction, I have remarked on several different strains: on Satis House as a dream or fairy-tale space with its own spell-casting witch; on the house as a school of repression for the Victorian adolescent; as a parody of the standard Victorian interior of the sort Benjamin wrote about; and as the site of a philosophical investigation of time. Considered together, these different themes create a powerful tonality for penetrating the barrier between reality and dream. In *Great Expectations,* the domestic interior itself becomes a "shining transparency" through which we see into the life of things.

Boffin's Bower

Great Expectations concludes in a scene on the desolate grounds of Satis House. Dickens's decision to change his original ending, which had been located on a street in London, may owe less to the influence of Bulwer-Lytton than to the endurance of the site of domesticity in his imagination: his addiction to dwelling. His last completed novel is without a ruling domestic space, and, as such, it becomes a novel about homelessness, or about the absence of a moral infrastructure in Victorian society.

The empty center of *Our Mutual Friend* is a society no longer given over to production and to the property that might be acquired with its proceeds, but to finance, speculation, and credit.[33] Mr. Lammle "is a gentleman of property. He invests his property" in "Shares"—or so people think—and perpetuates the fiction that he and his wife are building a house.[34] Overseas investments, short-term money markets, joint stock banking, and limited liability ventures keep the society of the novel unsteadily afloat. Around the ethical vacuum that this economy has created swirls one of the most inclusive populations Dickens ever created. The landed aristocracy, members of the older professions, the newly rich business class, the genteel hangers-on, the lower middle-class clerks and teachers, the small-business men and women, the working poor, the servants, the houseless, and the starving—all appear as so much detritus in a rushing stream. Neither thematically shaped into a duality of *haves* and *have nots* nor presented in terms of a hierarchy of class or work, or even a moral hierarchy of good and bad, the social world of *Our Mutual Friend* is constructed on a metaphysically condemned site in which all characters must acquire a moral existence or perish. The authorial generosity of the early novels, in which human eccentricity is affirmed with good humor, has been replaced by a narrator who effects the disappearance of characters out of disgust, like a disgruntled God: "And so, Lady Tippins, quite undetermined whether to-day is the day before yesterday, or the day after to-morrow, or the week after next, fades away," writes Dickens at the conclusion of one of the most surreal scenes in the novel: the expensive wedding of two people who do not know or love one another, who have almost no means of support, and who are being married in the home of a couple who barely know them, and who themselves will be insolvent within a year.[35]

The social context of this illusory state of affairs is a society that values nothing but money, and for that very reason is strangely uniform despite the disparities of class among its members. "Just as in money every qualitative difference between commodities is extinguished, so too for its part, as a radical leveler, it extinguishes all distinctions" writes Marx in *Capital*.[36] In *Our Mutual Friend* Dickens registers the emptying out of human content from human character that this "radical leveling" has brought about. The Veneerings' guests do not have names but labels that identify their value on the human stock exchange: "Boots and Brewer," "the Engineer," the "Member," the "thirty shillings a yard" bride, and so on. The theory of the embourgeoisement of society, whereby all classes increasingly identify with the money interests of the middle class, now underpins Dickens's vision of society.[37]

In *Our Mutual Friend* embourgeoisement does not lead to the social stability fantasized at the conclusions of earlier novels like *David Copperfield*. Instead, bourgeois houses and interiors, high and low, are associated with instability and decay. The lower-middle-class Wilfer house is beyond "Battle Bridge" in "a tract of suburban Sahara, where tiles and bricks were burnt, bones were boiled, carpets were beat, rubbish was hot, dogs were fought, and dust was heaped by contractors."[38] The house is under siege from within as well, as the daughter protests her misery: "I love money and want money. . . . I hate to be poor, and we are . . . beastly poor."[39] Tall, menacing mounds of dust darken the path to Boffin's Bower, which runs "between two lines of broken crockery."[40] Inside the Bower, not one domestic interior but two seem to compete for attention, as Boffin's attachment to lower-class comfort resists the encroachments of his wife's pretensions to middle-class fashion. At the Veneerings', the superficial guests are seen in their reflections in the mirror; at the Podsnaps', the timid daughter is in danger of being "crushed by the mere dead weight of Podsnappery,"[41] as if one of the Podsnaps' heavy pieces of furniture might fall on her. For domestic objects no longer have the aura of memory, as they do, for example, in *David Copperfield,* but only the luster of commodities. Even the bright and fresh "little cottage" that Bella and John Harmon (as Rokesmith) inhabit in the first months of their marriage, with its "prettiest of little breakfasts" laid out on a "snowy table-cloth," is merely a temporary abode and a deception, soon to be abandoned for a richer address.[42] And, unlike Agnes Wickfield, Bella assumes the bourgeois "angel in the house" role with considerable diffidence, studying books like *The Complete British Family Housewife* rather than taking to it naturally. The image of the woman as keeper of the keys, which may be traced back to Dutch genre painting, is disappearing in this last, brief vision of a "middle state" in Dickens, for the "little cottage" offers no more than the illusion of virtuous moderation, conjured by John Harmon, in a society that knows no limit of greed.

At the beginning of this chapter I suggested that the separation and distance between Dingley Dell and the Fleet in Dickens's first novel express the disjunction between the bourgeois domestic ideal and modern society in his imagination. In discussing Dickens's state of mind in his middle period, I portrayed Urania Cottage as Dickens's abortive effort to bring the two poles of his imagination together in the practical world. Throughout most of *Our Mutual Friend,* this duality has all but disappeared. As Silas Wegg discovers when given directions to Boffin's house, the path to Harmony Jail leads to Boffin's Bower. The Bower has not forgotten its origins in a jail: wealth is founded on tears and suffering, dust and death. In the following description, the economic source of the Boffins' interior is implied in the reference to "sawdust":

> It was the queerest of rooms, fitted and furnished more like a luxurious tap-room than anything else within the ken of Silas Wegg. . . . On the hob, a kettle steamed; on the hearth, a cat reposed. Facing the fire between the settles, a sofa, a footstool, and a little table formed a centerpiece devoted to Mrs. Boffin. They were garish in taste and colour, but were expensive articles of drawing-room furniture that had a very odd look beside the settles and the flaring gaslight pendent from the ceiling. There was a flowery carpet on the floor; but, instead of reaching to the fireside, its glowing vegetation stopped short at Mrs. Boffin's footstool, and gave place to a region of sand and sawdust. Mr. Wegg also noticed, with admiring eyes, that, while the flowery land displayed such hollow ornamentation as stuffed birds and waxen fruits under glass shades, there were, in the territory where vegetation ceased, compensatory shelves on which the best part of a large pie and likewise of a cold joint were plainly discernible among other solids.[43]

The "flowery carpet," "stuffed birds," and "waxen fruit under glass shades," illusory objects arranged to suggest unchangeable nature, exemplify what Adorno calls the "eternity" to which the bourgeois "condemns things."[44] Miss Havisham's neurotic impulse to stop time and preserve objects is here generalized to represent the very essence of bourgeois taste in decoration. Yet

Mrs. Boffin's "glowing vegetation . . . [gives] place to a region of sand and sawdust," an allusion to the origin of the Boffins' fortune in the dustheaps as well as to death itself, which encroaches on her illusions of eternal preservation.

At the end of the novel, Mrs. Boffin's pretensions appear to triumph as the Boffins abandon the Bower for the dustless Eden Bella and John Harmon inhabit, once John reveals his identity. The scene in which John takes his wife and newborn son to their luxurious new house with its "rainbow" colors borders on senile fantasy, as the Boffins "Mew, Quack-Quack, [and] Bow-Wow" at the door of the nursery, and eventually move in permanently, "exquisitely happy and daily cruising about to look at shops."[45] As suggested at the outset of this chapter, a dialectic of growth and decay is rooted in bourgeois history. The Boffins have a fortune to spend and they put their money to good use—they even purchase an orphan—but their money is putting *them* to use in turn. No longer dwellers, they have become shoppers, and Dickens ends the novel by placing them in an infantile consumer paradise.[46]

The Beloved Object and the Commodity

Dickens's unnerving return to his family after working at Warrens Blacking may help to account for the powerful aura of *things* in the novels. Many remembered objects had been lost to creditors, and cherished things that carried the poignant associations of his earlier years, like the crocodile book in *David Copperfield,* or even those that simply possessed the aura of familiarity, might have seemed slightly strange or uncanny. But it is the revolutionary transformation of objects in Victorian England mediated through this experience that most fully accounts for Dickens's evocation of the world of things.

Beloved objects that are found (Oliver's mother's wedding ring), or slowly recognized for what they are (her portrait), or treasured (David's book), are critical presences in the early novels and suggest the assimilation of subject and object that existed before the dominance of a market economy; fewer objects held particular meanings and memory-associations for their owners.[47] The increase in the sheer number of objects available for sale that characterizes a capitalist society is apparent in the proliferation of objects throughout the oeuvre, especially in the piled-up shops of the later novels. Together with changes in fashion, this increase disrupted the process of assimilation between people and things that held sway in earlier periods.[48] The treasured domestic objects of the earlier novels become the junk heaps of the later ones. As Boffin comments in *Our Mutual Friend,* "[T]here's some things that I never found among the dust."[49]

The luminous and protective interiors that well up in David Copperfield's memory reflect the earlier relation to things:

> The room was as neat as Janet or my aunt. As I laid down my pen, a moment since, to think of it, the air from the sea came blowing in again, mixed with the perfume of the flowers; and I saw the old-fashioned furniture brightly rubbed and polished, my aunt's inviolable chair and table by the round green fan in the bow window, the drugget-covered carpet, the cat, the kettle-holder, the two canaries, the old china, the punch-bowl full of dried rose leaves, the tall press guarding all sorts of bottles and pots, and, wonderfully out of keeping with the rest, my dusty self upon the sofa, taking note of everything.[50]

David and the things around him, subject and object, are absorbed into one another as David's eye ranges lovingly over each thing in the room. The room itself is compared to human character, as if it had a soul or personality. And David's "dustiness" is a mark of his own materiality, of what he shares with the material objects around him. Some of David's melancholy is owing to the fact that the things he loves will outlast him.

What marks Aunt Betsey's interior as pre-Victorian is its openness to the outside air as much as to the objects it contains. In contrast to the eerily preserved natural objects of Mrs Boffin, living birds and the odor of real flowers give this room a natural aura. Unlike the interiors of the later fiction, fewer objects are here given greater personal meaning. The phantasmagoria of the Meagleses' interior in *Little Dorrit* offers a powerful contrast.

"Mr Meagles led the way into the house," Dickens begins. "Some traces of the migratory habits of the family were to be observed in the covered frames and furniture, and wrapped-up hangings; but it was easy to see that it was one of Mr Meagles' whims to have the cottage always kept, in their absence, as if they were always coming back the day after to-morrow." After this introduction contrasting the mummified character of the interior with the restless habits of the Meagles, an elaborate, self-contained description of the interior follows:

> Of articles collected on his various expeditions, there was such a vast miscellany that it was like the dwelling of an amiable Corsair. There were antiquities from Central Italy, made by the best modern houses in that department of industry; bits of mummy from Egypt (and perhaps Birmingham); model gondolas from Venice; model villages from Switzerland; morsels of tessellated pavement from Herculaneum and Pompeii, like petrified minced veal; ashes out of tombs, and lava out of Vesuvius; Spanish fans, Spezzian straw hats, Moorish slippers, Tuscan hairpins, Carrera sculpture, Trastaverini scarves, Genoese velvets and filigree, Neapolitan coral, Roman cameos, Geneva jewellery, Arab lanterns, rosaries blest all round by the Pope himself, and an infinite variety of lumber. There were views, like and unlike, of a multitude of places; and there was one little picture-room devoted to a few of the regular sticky old Saints, with sinews like whipcord, hair like Neptune's, wrinkles like tattooing, and such coats of varnish that every holy personage served for a fly-trap, and became what is now called in the vulgar tongue a Catch-em-alive O. Of these pictorial acquisitions Mr Meagles spoke in the usual manner. He was no judge, he said,

except of what pleased himself; he had picked them up,
dirt-cheap, and people had considered them rather fine.

For the private individual, writes Benjamin, the interior "represents the universe." It is there that "he brings together remote locales and memories of the past. His living room is a box
in the theater of the world." Italy, Egypt, Switzerland, Spain,
and Morocco: Meagles would survey them all by means of the
art objects, miniatures, and fake antiquities purchased abroad
(though manufactured at home).[51] The world is contracted for
his "view," reduced to his own "picture-room," which is frozen
in time, always waiting to be repossessed, like the interior itself ("they were always coming back the day after tomorrow").
This spectacle is necessary to "sustain him in his illusions" of
historical connectedness and social importance and to suppress
the reality of his negligible social function in a capitalist economy.[52] Whence the "phantasmagoria" of the global interior: it
arises from the suppression Dickens hints at in the reference
to the "covered" and "wrapped-up" objects in Mr. Meagles's
room.

The Meagleses are no longer dwellers in a home full of
things with personal memory-associations, but those "migratory" creatures, bourgeois tourists, who have ransacked Europe
for commodities already infused with historical or religious
resonance. Fragments of the sacred litter their parlor, as if the
bourgeois interior had become a kind of clearinghouse for history itself. To Meagles, the economic potential of these items
is inversely validated by their cheapness: "he had picked them
up, dirt-cheap" but the fact that "people *had* considered them
rather fine" makes them investments. Meagles's elaborate display of "his spoils" is followed by yet another display: "When
he had shown all his spoils, Mr Meagles took them into his
own snug room overlooking the lawn, which was fitted up
in part like a dressing-room and in part like an office, and in
which, upon a kind of counter-desk, were a pair of brass scales
for weighing gold, and a scoop for shoveling out money."[53] To

Meagles, the source of his objects is neither their origins in a particular culture nor their human context in labor, but the cycle of exchange itself: "a pair of scales for weighing gold, and a scoop for shoveling out money." Located in the intimate space of his dressing room, where the sun rises and sets for the bourgeois individual, the scales and scoop represent both origin and destination.

No longer a home, the bourgeois interior has become an imperial masquerade of trophies gathered from afar, evidence of the transformation of all cultural values into a world of exchange. In Marx's words: "Everything becomes salable and purchasable. Circulation becomes the great social retort into which everything is thrown, to come out again as money crystal. Nothing is immune from this alchemy, the bones of the saints cannot withstand it."[54] The "sticky old saints" in Meagles's parlor attract flies. Dickens's description is of course highly comic, but the contents of Meagles's house are in keeping with the negative social vision of *Little Dorrit,* in which the "circumlocution office," symbolic of the ubiquity of exchange, is "the great social retort" to human creativity.[55] Benjamin writes of the "nihilism . . . [at] the innermost core of bourgeois coziness":

> Nineteenth-century domestic interior. The space disguises itself—puts on, like an alluring creature, the costume of moods. The self-satisfied burgher should know something of the feeling that the next room might have witnessed the coronation of Charlemagne as well as the assassination of Henry IV, the signing of the Treaty of Verdun as well as the wedding of Otto and Theophano. In the end, things are merely mannequins, and even the great moments of world history are only costumes beneath which they exchange glances of complicity with nothingness, with the petty and the banal. Such nihilism is the innermost core of bourgeois coziness. . . . To live in these interiors was to have woven a dense fabric about oneself within a spider's

web, in whose toils world events hang loosely suspended like so many insect bodies sucked dry.[56]

The sickened spirit of the Victorian bourgeois is implied in a statement Meagles makes to Clennam just before the passage describing his interior. Alluding to their first meeting in Marseilles, "'Lord bless me!'" he cries, "rubbing his hands in relish, 'it was an uncommonly pleasant thing being in quarantine, wasn't it?'"[57]

The Smell and Spell of
"Things" in Henry James's
The Spoils of Poynton

"I've a great respect for *things*!" exclaims the dubious Madame Merle in Henry James's *The Portrait of a Lady* (1881). "[W]e're each of us made up of some cluster of appurtenances." As for the "self," she continues, "Where does it begin? Where does it end? It overflows into everything that belongs to us—and then it flows back again. . . . One's self—for other people—is one's expression of one's self; and one's house, one's furniture, one's garments, the books one reads, the company one keeps—these things are all expressive."[1]

It would be difficult to find a more succinct statement of the philosophical presuppositions of nineteenth-century novelistic realism. That James would ultimately break from this tradition is suggested in the mere fact that it is the questionable Madame Merle who defends the view of life that "realism" expresses. Merlin-like Madame Merle possesses almost uncanny powers of deception, and James's ambivalence toward his Balzacian creation suggests a simultaneous attraction to and distrust of realism itself—an ambivalence directly relevant to the subject of the domestic interior. As one of the prime settings of the realist novel, the domestic interior will necessarily undergo changes if the materialist view of life, upon which realism supposedly rests, is challenged.

I say "supposedly" because if we look again at Madame Merle's words, we may notice how easily they metamorphose into something quite different from a straightforward affirmation of the power of empirical reality to provide us with data to interpret. If the living self "overflows" into matter (and, even

more mysteriously, "flows back again" to the "self"), if furnishings are "expressive," are objects then alive—alive in ways
that cannot be rationally articulated? This question, already
hinted at in Austen's description of the objects in Fanny's room
and comically presented in talking objects in Dickens, is the
philosophical subject of *The Spoils of Poynton* (1897), a novella
that centers on three domestic interiors, two of which contain
objects inhabited by spirits. Many of James's earlier works of
course portray interiors, some of which, like Dr. Sloper's residence in *Washington Square,* are dynamic presences. (When
Morris Townsend visits the house while Catherine and her father are abroad, the luxurious interior acts on him in such a
way that his financial expectations rise.) But *The Spoils of Poynton* marks an advance in James's self-conscious exploration of
the bourgeois interior; it is also generally recognized as crucial
to James's development as a novelist, although the animation
of objects in the story has received less critical attention than
one might expect.[2] It would seem that James's critics are less
open than he was to the possibility that spirits might be alive
in objects. Yet this openness, as we shall see, may have been a
catalyst to his artistic development.

I shall return to James's artistic development at the end of
this chapter, after considering the subject of "things" in a historical context and in the novella. James himself found an ex-
cessive attention to "things" in fiction slightly vulgar; Balzac's
universe, he said, "fairly smells too much of them . . . [T]he
larger ether, the diviner air, is in peril of finding among them
scarce room to circulate." *The Spoils of Poynton* may be read as
James's effort to free himself from the *smell* of things (their vulgar association with what he calls "the machinery of life, of
its furniture and fittings")[3] without sacrificing their *spell* (their
seemingly magical aura, their capacity to embody the essence
of human feeling and thought).

Society itself smelled of "things" in the nineteenth century.
According to Asa Briggs, the Victorians "widened the range
of things much further than any previous century, eventually

reshaping all earlier versions of economics to explain 'demand' more fully than supply." Briggs cites the "marginal utility economics" of Philip Wicksteed, who, in contrast to "classical" economists like Ricardo, Mill, or Marx, concentrates on the vast number of desirable objects that enter into a "'circle of exchange' based on choice."[4] By presenting the individual with an excess of objects from which to choose, the huge increase and availability of manufactured domestic products disrupted the relation between people and things that had existed in earlier eras; before this great proliferation took place, fewer objects held more meaning. In the last chapter, I treated this phenomenon in its psychological aspect—for example, in calling attention to the motif of lost objects in Dickens's novels. To lose a treasured object is to lose a part of oneself. But there is another loss to be considered: the loss to civilization of the domestic arts and crafts that often produced the treasured objects that were handed down through generations and that mass production replaced.

In the work of William Morris, father of the arts and crafts movement in interior design, we see one response to this loss.[5] Morris aimed to restore to the interior the traditional skills of carpenters, stonemasons, weavers, and apprentices that had flourished for centuries before mass production rendered them obsolete. He himself learned the lost art of tapestry weaving from an old French book published before the French Revolution—the last school of tapestry weaving in England had been closed in the eighteenth century—and his own textile and wallpaper designs show the influence of the old tapestries (see "Windrush," opposite). Reacting against the mediocrity of manufactured products, Morris established the firm Morris, Marshall, Faulkner & Company in the early 1860s, between the publication dates of *Little Dorrit* and *Our Mutual Friend*. Morris had interiors like those of Meagles and Boffin in mind when he attacked popular decoration and luxury in his public lectures. He believed the houses being built for wealthy industrialists

"Windrush" fabric, ca. 1883, by William Morris. Morris delighted in the sensuous particularity and "smell" of things. By all accounts, he was never happier than when bent over a vat of dye soaking one of his handwoven fabrics. Inspired by fifteenth-century Italian and Near Eastern textile patterns, "Windrush" was printed at Merton Abbey. (Courtesy of the Museum of Fine Arts, Boston)

(whom he called "ignorant, purse-proud digesting machines"), designed for the sake of show alone, were places where it would be impossible to lead a "calm, dignified, and therefore happy life."[6] Civilization had come to mean, not the attainment of ideals, but "more stuffed chairs and more cushions, and more carpets and gas."[7] To Morris, the domestic interior was the medium for a utopian social vision: the site of beautiful objects crafted by human, not mechanical, energies, the opportunity to express what Thomas Carlyle had called "the inward primary powers of man," of man as "creator and producer."[8]

This background is important to understanding James's novella because it suggests how much was at stake in matters of interior decoration when Victorian civilization entered the modern period.[9] The "spoils" of Poynton may be understood to mean several things in the story—fine taste, bourgeois greed, the plunder of battle—but one thing they quite literally represent is a palpable, living past—specifically, the domestic arts and crafts embodied in furnishings of earlier periods. James said that he was originally drawn to the story that formed the basis of *The Spoils of Poynton,* the story of a struggle between a mother and son for a houseful of rare furnishings, for the light it might shed on "the fierce appetite" for the furnishings "of the more labouring ages."[10] He originally intended for the "things" to "form the very center" of the story's "crisis." They would do justice to "the great array in which Balzac . . . would have marshaled them" and would possess a "common consciousness." While "not directly articulate," they had "wondrous things to say." The tactic of giving voice to the objects was abandoned, however, not only on the grounds of its unlikely appeal to an editor, but because it would have been too "costly" for James himself "to keep up," insofar as it would have diminished other voices. Instead, he placed Fleda Vetch in the foreground, a character who "almost demonically both sees and feels" the "radiant . . . light" emanating from the things.[11] In the final version of the story, the things themselves are sentient, but they are only vaguely described, and Fleda's consciousness of them takes center stage.

On the simplest and perhaps the most profound level, James's story is about one woman's hysterical response to the loss of this living past. Mrs. Gereth's hysteria takes the form of fetishism, an irrational devotion to the beautiful objects of Poynton, and a profound aversion to the philistine taste that seems to threaten what she values so highly. The sight of the interior of Waterbath, the vulgar house of the Brigstocks, causes her to weep and "her face to burn" because she fears that its owners will ultimately have control over her precious objects. The great friendship between Mrs. Gereth and Fleda is founded on mutual taste, or on a conspiracy of judgment against the bad taste of the Brigstocks' interior:

The house was bad in all conscience, but it might have
passed if [the Brigstocks] had only let it alone. This saving mercy was beyond them; they had smothered it with
trumpery ornament and scrapbook art, with strange excrescences and bunchy draperies, with gimcracks that
might have been keepsakes for maid-servants and non-
descript conveniences that might have been prizes for
the blind. They had gone wildly astray over carpets and
curtains; they had an infallible instinct for disaster, and
were so cruelly doom-ridden that it rendered them almost tragic. Their drawing-room, Mrs. Gereth lowered
her voice to mention, caused her face to burn, and each
of the new friends confided to the other that in her own
apartment she had given way to tears. There was in the
elder lady's a set of comic water-colors, a family joke by a
family genius, and in the younger's a souvenir from some
centennial or other Exhibition, that they shudderingly alluded to. The house was perversely full of souvenirs of
places even more ugly than itself and of things it would
have been a pious duty to forget. The worst horror was
the acres of varnish, something advertised and smelly,
with which everything was smeared.[12]

More horrors are detailed later in the story when Fleda recol-
lects visiting a conservatory with "a stuffed cockatoo fastened
to a tropical bough and a waterless fountain composed of shells
stuck into some hardened paste."[13]

With its smelly smears of varnish covering "excrescences,"
the interior of Waterbath is enough to make one retch—or is
it Vetch?—an association I shall take up later. Echoing the
Veneerings' sticky residence in *Our Mutual Friend*, James's description raises the nineteenth-century interior to new heights
of comic disgust. Yet the presence of lonely, meditative Fleda
tempers the comedy. She too shudders at the "intimate ugliness" of the interior, just as, later in the story, she gasps and
rolls her "dilated eyes" at the beauty of Poynton.[14] This un-

dertow of hysteria—of winces, gasps, shudders, and cries that border on shrieks[15]—prevails in *The Spoils of Poynton,* making the tragic mishap of the plot inevitable. Reacting prematurely to the possibility of an engagement between Fleda and her son, Mrs. Gereth returns the treasured objects to Poynton before the engagement is secure; Mona reclaims Owen, and Fleda is sacrificed.

The susceptibility of Fleda and Mrs. Gereth to fetishism, rather than to some other type of mental condition, may be the result of sexual repression—it is easy to argue this on the basis of details in the story—but the traditional psychoanalytic explanation of the cause of hysteria need not negate the authenticity of the two women's response to the loss of a living past.[16] In other words, we might speculate that Morris's response to the loss of domestic arts was less neurotic or more productive than that of James's characters, but it arose from the same reality. Just as Morris wished to recreate the past, the women desire to hold, look at, and touch the past by means of the objects. The past is gone, but the spoils remain.

The fetishism that possesses Mrs. Gereth is that of the aesthete, and James lends credence to it by making the things themselves genuine fetishes—that is, objects invested with magical powers: "In the watches of the night" at Ricks, after the things of Poynton are removed there, Fleda senses that the pieces "around her seemed to suffer like chopped limbs. To lie there in the stillness was partly to listen for some soft low plaint from them."[17] After they are returned to Poynton, the objects experience the "joy" of "recover[ing] their own."[18] The idea of the fetish at work in these sentences predates Freud's appropriation of the term as sexual perversion and Marx's concept of "commodity fetishism." Associated with the earliest forms of religion, it is a more ancient concept even than the commodity, insofar as the latter word is used to refer to an article of exchange in the marketplace. Although both the Freudian and Marxist concepts of fetishism have occupied the attention of James critics in recent years, the primitive association of fetishism with magic in the story has been neglected.[19] Yet the history of the word *fetish,* which James may have known (although he doesn't use the word in the story), deserves attention. According to the anthropologist William Pietz, the word was probably first used in the early sixteenth century by the Portuguese, who, exploring the coast of Africa, found natives using small material objects in their religious worship. The word was applied to the idols and amulets made by hand and supposed to possess magical powers.[20] One of the most evocative fetishes at Poynton is the crucifix of ivory found in Malta, a country that throughout history has played a vital role in the interplay between emerging Europe and the older cultures of Africa. James makes a point of the fact that the crucifix is not a Maltese cross in a technical sense—that is, not the eight-pointed cross that dates back to the first crusade—but a cross *from* Malta, as if to lay emphasis on its archaic origins. Like another Maltese fetish, the Maltese falcon in the John Huston film, the cross "was at last unearthed," we are told, after a clue as to its whereabouts is "followed through mazes of secrecy."[21]

Mrs. Gereth's battle with Mona is fierce not because she has any feeling for her son—Fleda remarks on the utter absence of maternal tenderness—but because her own fetishism is matched by the different but equally powerful fetishism of the Brigstocks: what Marx called "commodity fetishism," the process by which objects, entering the cycle of exchange, are abstracted from the human labor that produced them. As Bill Brown and others have pointed out, commodity fetishism peaked in America in the 1880s and 1890s, in part because of the widespread use of advertising. Waterbath shares with the bourgeois houses discussed earlier, those of the Boffins and Meagles, an array of commodities purchased abroad—including those objects of manufactured remembrance, "souvenirs"[22]—and the morbid taste for preserving or representing natural objects in some sort of ideal, petrified state. The stuffed cockatoo fastened to a tropical bough creates the illusion that one is in some sort of paradise, above the cycle of exchange, above even the fallen human world.

Mrs. Gereth's fetishism is as different from that of the Brigstocks as Poynton is from Waterbath. The objects she has gathered together represent a triumph of exquisite taste; Poynton is a veritable work of art reflecting "the genius, the passion, the patience of the collector."[23] Decidedly not bourgeois in taste—it accentuates architectural features rather than "smother[ing]" them with wallpaper and varnish and, like aristocratic Pemberley, "contradicted gardeners and refined on nature"[24]—Poynton nonetheless possesses one of the defining characteristics of the nineteenth-century bourgeois interior: it has been put together by its owners for *effect,* to be displayed, admired, and judged. When she visits Poynton, Mrs. Brigstock turns up the underside of plates and taps porcelain cups, and Mrs. Gereth doesn't demur; she has collected the things of Poynton because of their aesthetic value and both expects and desires them to be judged. She lives apart from Poynton for much of the year, admiring it at a distance as a work of art rather than longing for it as a home.

Mrs. Gereth's unwillingness to deliver Poynton into the philistine hands of Mona Brigstock arises from no mere "crude love of possession," but from the unwillingness of the artist to be alienated from her art, the laborer from her labor, the collector from her collection.[25] The individual pieces of Poynton are fetishized commodities in the Marxist sense, but the composition of Poynton as a whole is the labor of love of Mrs. Gereth, and James wants us to recognize the value of this kind of labor as well as the consummate achievement of the collector in detaching objects from their use-value and integrating them "into a new, expressly devised historical system: the collection." As Benjamin writes, "for the collector, the world is present, and indeed ordered, in each of his objects."[26] "Poynton was the record of a life. It was written in great syllables of color and form, the tongues of other countries and the hands of rare artists."[27] The French and Italian furnishings, the Oriental china, the Jacobean architecture, the English landscaping—all work together to create a cosmopolitan aesthetic composition of incomparable effect.[28] To remove or divide the collection, to disturb the composition in any way, is to destroy its aesthetic integrity and its significance as the historical "record of a life." For this reason Mrs. Gereth wishes to pass on the house and collection whole and entire to someone who will care for and protect it: "It was absolutely unselfish—she cared nothing for mere possession. She thought solely and incorruptibly of what was best for the things."[29] When the "things" are transplanted to Ricks, they lose their beauty, and when left in the careless hands of Mona and Owen, they are destroyed by the fire.

At the same time that James invites us to acknowledge Mrs. Gereth's "genius for composition"[30] and to respect her clairvoyance as to the fate of the "things," he invites us to judge her. Like Browning's dangerous aesthete, the Duke of Ferrara (another fetishist of art who obsesses over an object that seems to be alive and to look back at him), Mrs. Gereth never descends, never "stoops": "What struck Fleda most in [Poynton] was the high pride of her friend's taste, a fine arrogance, a sense of style . . . never compromised nor stooped."[31] Mrs. Gereth has given herself to a passion for beautiful things and created a domestic museum that is a record of her own life, a life without suffering and therefore without ghosts: "Somehow there were no ghosts at Poynton," comments Fleda after Mrs. Gereth has lost her battle with Mona, "That was the only fault."[32] Poynton's only drawback, then, reflects Mrs. Gereth's own failure to acknowledge the human. "The truth was simply that all Mrs. Gereth's scruples were on one side and that her ruling passion had in a manner despoiled her of her humanity."[33] It is as if her "humanity" had seeped into the objects themselves.

The descriptions of Poynton and Waterbath resonate with controversies of taste and value that preceded James. In "The Philosophy of Furniture" (1840), Edgar Allan Poe defined bad taste in furnishings in descriptions of interiors that sound like

Waterbath. An "extensive volume of drapery of any kind is, under any circumstance, irreconcilable with good taste," he wrote. "The abomination of flowers, or representations of well-known objects of any kind, should not be endured within the limits of Christendom."[34] Poe's "philosophy of furniture" is not unlike his "philosophy of composition," as expounded in the well-known essay by that title published six years later, which commences with "the consideration of *effect*."[35] As in art, insisted Poe, well-furnished interiors must observe "undeviating principles which regulate all varieties of art; and very nearly the same laws by which we decide on the higher merits of painting, suffice for decision on the adjustment of the chamber."[36] The nineteenth-century movement in interior decoration seems to have possessed the chameleonlike ability to take on the coloring of surrounding movements; as Poe's statements suggest, it overlapped with the rise of aesthetic criticism, which had originated in Germany in the late eighteenth century, just as it would later merge with socialist thought in the work of William Morris.[37] Morris lectured in London in the 1870s and 1880s, and Oscar Wilde, elaborating on Morris's ideas, wove the different strands of aesthetics, politics, and house decoration together on lecture tour in America in 1882.

At the root of much of this discourse was the inspirational aestheticism of John Ruskin, whom James met in 1869. "Taste is not only a part and an index of morality," Ruskin lectured in "Traffic" (1864), "it is the ONLY morality. The first, and last, and closest trial question to any living creature is, 'What do you like?' Tell me what you like, and I'll tell you what you are."[38] The Brigstocks reveal themselves in their poor taste—they are as banal as their house—but their crassness is matched by Mrs. Gereth's brutality. As Oscar Wilde said, "There is nothing sane about the worship of beauty"—and Mrs. Gereth's passion for beautiful objects has reduced her capacity to feel to little more than a maniacal protectiveness for the things of Poynton: She "thrust in everywhere the question of 'things' . . . read all behavior in the light of some fancied relation to them."[39] She is as indifferent to human nature as, in Ruskin's eyes, the aesthetic perfection of Poynton proclaims her to be. (In *The Stones of Venice,* Ruskin had railed against the pursuit of an inhuman perfectionism in art.) "What had her whole life been but an effort toward completeness and perfection?"[40]

James is sounding familiar Victorian themes or ideas in the story, but he is also working to free himself from the powerful intellectual legacy they represent. Like Ruskin, Tennyson, Browning, and other Victorians coming before him, for example, he shows how the aesthetic sense, operating independently of everything else, can "despoil" us of our "humanity." Owen and Fleda are frequently bruised by Mrs. Gereth's insensitivity, much in the way a reader of Matthew Arnold encounters with a shock the well-known "Wragg" passage from his defense of aesthetic criticism. Relative to Ruskin, Arnold would stand at the opposite end of the Victorian spectrum of ideas on art. After reading his enemies' eulogies of England as "the best [society] in the whole world," Arnold describes how he came upon a passage in the newspaper about "a girl named Wragg" who had murdered her child. "*Wragg*!" exclaims Arnold. "If we are to talk of ideal perfection, of 'the best in the whole world,' has anyone reflected what a touch of grossness in our race, what an original short-coming in the more delicate spiritual perceptions, is shown by the natural growth amongst us of such hideous names, —Higginbottom, Stiggins, Bugg!"[41] What is startling about the passage is Arnold's evident blindness or indifference to the impression his distaste might make on the reader. To draw back in aesthetic disgust over the name of the criminal rather than in horror at the crime of infanticide calls into question, to say the least, the "delicate spiritual perceptions" of Arnold himself. In *The Spoils of Poynton,* James is more cannily aware of his audience's response, and he directs us to doubt the delicate spiritual perceptions of Mrs. Gereth, not his own. Yet in choosing a questionable name like *Vetch* for his most admirable character, a name that is almost as unrefined as Wragg, and in exposing sensations of aesthetic disgust with which the Jamesian reader is likely to be in sympathy—who can doubt that Waterbath is hideous?—James playfully engages the Arnoldian spirit of distaste. Ruskin had demanded that we see true beauty as a moral quality, but Arnold's ultimate (and unintended) project, as T. S. Eliot saw, was to separate the aesthetic and the moral—whence Arnold's confidence in indulging a purely aesthetic response to a human tragedy. In James's story, Fleda is the Ruskinian: she sees the moral and human presence in the aunt's taste and therefore sees its beauty. Mrs. Gereth is the Arnoldian (or Paterian) aesthete: she sees only that the aesthetic of Ricks is inferior to that of Poynton. When the two women come together in the aunt's house, James effects a compromise between the two points of view. With her ingenious taste, Mrs. Gereth improves the aunt's interior, and the morally delicate Fleda approves. The Victorian tension between aesthetics and ethics is quietly resolved.

The name *Vetch* is questionable because it rhymes with *retch,* whereas *Adela Gereth* possesses an almost musical mellifluousness. The words *Fleda Vetch* together suggest the two opposing tendencies explored in the story: to fly and to retch, transcendence and descent, spirit and matter, beauty and ugliness, admiration and disgust, Poynton and Waterbath—and, we might also add, Ruskin and Arnold (or Walter Pater, the figure around whom these controversies raged in the latter quarter of the nineteenth century). In *The Spoils of Poynton,* these extremes are dialectically related in that Poynton and Waterbath prove to have more in common with one another than either has with the third and finally more humane option of Ricks, just as Ruskin and Arnold share assumptions that neither shares with Henry James. For all of Arnold's aestheticism, he believed in the potential of art "to console us, to sustain us" as religion had in the past;[42] he possessed a characteristically Victorian confidence in the benevolence of art that James does not share. After Fleda gives up all hope of marrying the man she loves, "her obliterated passion" is revived by the thought of the art objects residing at Poynton. She "thought of them hour after hour"

and they bring her a "strange peace."[43] But James takes care
to demolish the hope that art will "console" and "sustain" her.
The art objects are destroyed by the fire, and the last sentence
of the story—"I'll go back"—announces Fleda's retreat from
this hope.

Fleda has a home now; however, she will retreat to Ricks. In
the year *The Spoils of Poynton* was published, James himself was
searching for what he called a "lowly refuge,"[44] which he found
in Lamb House at Rye. "I have . . . taken, a couple of months
ago, a little old house in the country—for the rest of my days!"
he wrote to his sister in December of 1897.[45] James's life of
renunciation at Lamb House, where he "suffered for want of
[London's] social [and] . . . intellectual air"[46] at the same time
that he produced his three last novels, bears affinities to Fleda's
celibate existence. Here is the interior of the deceased maiden
aunt, as described earlier in the story:

> The house was crowded with objects of which the aggre-
> gation somehow made a thinness and the futility a grace;
> things that told her they had been gathered as slowly and
> as lovingly as the golden flowers of Poynton. She too, for
> a home, could have lived with them: they made her fond
> of the old maiden-aunt. . . . The poor lady had had some
> tender little story; she had been sensitive and ignorant
> and exquisite: that too was a sort of origin, a sort of at-
> mosphere for relics and rarities, though different from the
> sorts most prized at Poynton. . . . [I]t wasn't a question
> of love, now, for these [objects]: it was only a question
> of a certain practical patience. . . . [S]he was so sure [the
> maiden-aunt] had deeply suffered.[47]

Later, after Mrs. Gereth takes possession of Ricks, Fleda notices again "the impression, somehow, of something dreamed
and missed, something reduced, relinquished, resigned" in the
house's interior: "the poetry, as it were, of something sensibly
gone." "Ah," she comments at last, "there's something here that
will never be in the inventory! . . . It's a kind of fourth dimen-

sion. It's a presence, a perfume, a touch. It's a soul, a story, a
life."

In this declaration and in the passage that follows it, we encounter the deepest form of fetishism in the story, the fetishism
that freed James from the Balzacian smell of things without
sacrificing their *spell:* their capacity to embody the essence of
human thought and feeling. Fleda attributes conscious life to
the objects in the aunt's interior. They mediate between the
visible and the spirit worlds; through them, the deceased aunt
speaks. Fleda continues:

> "There's ever so much more here than you and I. We're
> in fact just three!"
> "Oh, if you count the ghosts!"
> "Of course I count the ghosts. It seems to me ghosts
> count double—for what they were and for what they
> are."

The ghosts have made their presence known through objects
that, like those in Miss Havisham's house, act as a veil or "shining transparency" between the past and the present. Penetrating the levels of time, they make it possible for Fleda and her
new pupil, Mrs. Gereth, to see into the past. There is a sense in
which this vision confers on both characters a certain peace, cur-
ing them of their hysteria: "Mrs. Gereth met her eyes awhile.
'Goose!' she quietly remarked as she turned away. There was a
curtness in it; nevertheless it represented a considerable part of
the basis of their new life." Taste, which had earlier exercised
a tyranny and was the focus of hysterical desires and aversions,
is now a question of the "air" or spirit. Of the aunt's presence
Fleda cryptically remarks that "it's in the very taste of the
air!"[48] James's original intention to animate objects in the story
therefore remains central to its meaning, despite the fact that
Fleda's consciousness is the means by which we come to know
them. She is in the driver's seat, but they are telling her where
to go. Like the objects Proust worships as Diana Fuss describes
them, the aunt's things are "fetishistic signs of the simultane-

ous absence and presence of the dead," steadfastly refusing the forward movement of time.[49]

After Owen is married, Fleda herself claims to be "happy," and, before the final scene of the story, we believe this to be possible. She has managed to position herself between flight and descent, as her name suggests; the animistic objects among which she lives are a sign of this reconciliation of spirit and matter. In moral terms, the reconciliation is apparent as well: she has plighted her troth to Owen's integrity, as it were, but has given way neither to the dishonorable act of "letting herself go" to acquire him as a husband together with Poynton, nor to the self-deception of believing that her reluctance to do so was motivated solely by moral scruples. There is a sense in which Fleda is more suited to be the companion of Mrs. Gereth than of Owen, largely because James conceives of her sexual inhibition as an aspect of her intelligence and spiritual refinement. (Mona can "let herself go" because she is coarse and unintelligent.)

The melodramatic ending of *The Spoils of Poynton,* in which the house goes up in flames, threatens to compromise the fine ambivalence of this resolution, in which Fleda appears to be contented with living out her life as a spinster among a spinster's ghosts, for it momentarily returns the operations of the story to its nineteenth-century context, not only in Victorian melodrama but theology. Fleda travels to Poynton to retrieve her gift from Owen and, just as it is left open whether or not she will choose the Maltese cross, symbol of her own and Owen's sacrifice, the story ends on a question of being saved:

> She heard herself repeat mechanically, yet as if asking for the first time: "Poynton's *gone?*"
> The man hesitated. "What can I call it, miss, if it ain't really saved?"[50]

Fleda's hard-won equilibrium between transcendence and descent is here recast in the rather obvious symbolism of Christian salvation. As in Browning's "doctrine of the imperfect" (a poetic version of the architectural aesthetic of Ruskin's *The Stones of Venice*), a realm beyond the human, a divine Christian realm, proves to be the context for the *vita nuova* that Fleda achieves in the story: the balance between her idealism or desire to rise and do what is right (she wishes to preserve Owen's honor in the form of his engagement to another woman) and her humble acknowledgment of imperfection (she desperately loves and wants him nonetheless). "[A] man's reach should exceed his grasp," says Browning's Andrea del Sarto, "Or what's a Heaven for?"[51] Seeking is finding, and Fleda has gone to Poynton to seek the cross—Christianity has its fetishes too—and the destruction of the Maltese cross together with all of the art objects in the fire presumably cures her of her art worship by proclaiming the ephemeral nature of all material things.

Yet the heightened ambiguity of language that characterizes the end of the story works against the Christian melodrama. "[I]n the house the house was all," Fleda thinks as she approaches "the great interior she had been haunting," consumed by "the thought that all for Fleda Vetch . . . the house was standing there."[52] Fleda yearns to realize herself in "the great interior"—now a metaphor for existence itself—as if she herself were a ghost. Does the house haunt her or does she haunt the house? In placing his character on metaphysically uncertain terrain, James prepares the way for the later novels in which metaphysical-moral questions of transcendence and descent are elaborated further. As the title *The Wings of the Dove* alone suggests, these questions become central to the later novels, and in *The Golden Bowl* James considerably extends his examination of how they figure in the fetish. The golden bowl gathers to itself many of the properties of the fetishized objects in *The Spoils of Poynton.* In the "little shop," the dealer describes the gold on the bowl:

> "You couldn't scrape it off—it has been too well put on; put on . . . by some very fine old worker and by some beautiful old process."

Charlotte, frankly charmed with the cup, smiled back at him now. "A lost art?"

"Call it a lost art."

"But of what time then is the whole thing?"

"Well, say also of a lost time."

The girl considered. "Then if it's so precious, how comes it to be cheap?"[53]

The loss and cheapening of a living past in art, the capacity of objects to penetrate levels of time: these themes, as we have seen, are developed in *The Spoils of Poynton,* but they are developed without precise details as to the objects themselves. With only a few exceptions, such as the Maltese cross, the actual contents of Poynton and Ricks remain vague, whereas the vulgar, factory-made products of Waterbath, like the stuffed cockatoo on the tropical bough, are particularized. Presumably, when objects successfully embody aesthetic and spiritual ideals they can only be revealed through what is *not* said. Described in their sensuous particularity, they have too much of the Balzacian smell of life, the Dickensian smell of rot and decay.

In *The Golden Bowl,* in which James is directly concerned with investigating the spiritual properties of matter, the material properties of spirit, he is bolder.[54] He leaves behind the materialist social world of the bourgeoisie, which had been a subject of *The Spoils of Poynton,* and focuses on a single, beautiful, symbolic material object, describing all aspects of it in detail and elaborating the characters, themes, and actions of the novel around it. There are no bourgeois interiors in *The Golden Bowl,* not only because the main characters are above the middle classes but also because descriptive details of domestic interiors are kept at a minimum. The sole survivor of the catalogue of objects, one of the hallmarks of the tradition of novelistic realism going back to *Robinson Crusoe,* is the bowl itself. For James, the "smell of things" is disappearing, and, with it, the rich palpability of the domestic interior, that inventory of "real" objects through which the first bourgeois in

English fiction heroically and absurdly lay claim to civilization in a cave. This would seem to mark almost too great a loss to fiction, were it not for the grandeur of what followed: the modernist works of Proust, Joyce, Woolf, Kafka, Bergman, and others, in which the bourgeois domestic interior becomes a medium for memory and dream. For memories and dreams are no less powerful for being odorless.

Virginia Woolf and
the Passing of Victorian
Domesticity

The fate of Poynton in James's story suggests the imperiled state of the Victorian home. It is almost as if Poynton were "unable to survive the passage to Modernity,"[1] so rooted is it in what James called the "Old Things" of the past. Howards End, in E. M. Forster's novel by that name, also has difficulty making the transition to modernity and does so only after sacrificing its bourgeois character. At the end of *Howards End* (1910) an unconventional family—an illegitimate child its heir—has replaced the traditional family that once occupied the domestic interior. In *To the Lighthouse,* published seventeen years after *Howards End,* a house deteriorates with the death of the Victorian mother, and the world is reimagined by an unmarried woman artist who lives in rooms "off the Brompton Road" that we never see.[2]

After World War I, the bourgeois home as mythological configuration came to an end. While the bourgeois class continued in full force, the domestic interior was reconceived by the antibourgeois energies of Bloomsbury, as recent work on the Omega workshops, the design collective active between 1913 and 1919, has shown.[3] The domestic interior now becomes the *explicit* imaginative space, or space for experimentation in living, that earlier novelists had shown us it always implicitly was. As the art historian Christopher Reed suggests, Bloomsbury painters and writers attempted to create domestic environments suitable to their aspirations for new and unconventional ways of life.[4]

In the domain of architecture, Le Corbusier launched another sort of attack on the Victorian interior. First appearing in the 1920s, Le Corbusier's writings articulate the modernist antagonism to the conventional function of the Victorian home as a private refuge. With their lightness, airiness, and continuity of inner and outer space, his buildings defied the monumentality of the Victorian home and its protectively enclosed interior.[5] If the Corbusian metaphor for the house is industrial, a "machine for living in," the Victorian metaphor for the home is organic. "The traces of its inhabitants are molded into the interior," writes Benjamin.[6] The Victorian interior wears the physiognomy of its occupants, especially its female occupants.

As we have seen, domestic space was not always the provenance of the woman. Robinson Crusoe is identified with his well-stocked cave, Darcy with the tasteful furnishings of Pemberley, but in the process of industrialization the husband's labor was removed from the home and the specifically feminine domesticity of the Victorians arose.[7] As industrial management came to dominate the work life of middle- and upper-class men, "so the family, and by extension the house, expanded in tandem to act as an emotional counterweight." The home became "the source of refuge and retreat but also strength and renewal,"[8] its regenerative emotional energies arising from what Coventry Patmore called "the angel in the house." In his best-selling work by that name, Patmore describes the domestic angel as the "aim" and the "epitome" of womanhood, a figure who typifies the entire gender.[9] The publication of *The Angel in the House* (1854–62) was closely followed in 1865 by John Ruskin's brilliantly evocative "Of Queens' Gardens," an immensely popular didactic essay that likewise characterized woman's intellect as peculiarly suited to the private sphere. A more resounding voice than that of Patmore, Ruskin enjoyed great prestige in England and abroad and was admired by writers of the generation coming after him, Virginia Woolf among them.[10] When Ruskin claimed that woman's exalted role was to perpetuate civilization through her benevolent and moral influence over men, people took note. If not for her, he warned, civilized life would fall to ruin.[11]

In many ways this is exactly what happens in *To the Light-house.* Without Mrs. Ramsey, the house, the family, and the little social world she has created around her all fall apart. The physical deterioration of the house is strikingly narrated after her death: "The swallows nested in the drawing-room; the floor was strewn with straw; the plaster fell in shovelfuls; rafters were laid bare; rats carried off this and that to gnaw behind the wainscots."[12] The type of bourgeois womanhood that Mrs. Ramsey represents is so closely identified with the life of the domestic interior that her departure from the cultural scene signals the rapid decay of domesticity itself. It is as if the domestic interior had become the medium of energies so overcharged that it comes close to self-immolation. Although this fate is averted by the domestic labor of the two crones, Mrs. McNab and Mrs. Bast, Woolf makes it clear that the house will never be the same without the likes of Mrs. Ramsey to inhabit it. Two years after the publication of the novel, Woolf wrote: "For women have sat indoors all these millions of years, so that by this time the very walls are permeated by their creative force, which has, indeed, so overcharged the capacity of bricks and mortar that it must needs harness itself to pens and brushes and business and politics."[13] Before we consider the redirection of feminine creativity in the final section of *To the Lighthouse,* when Lily completes her painting and has her "vision," we may well ask: who or what was the force that could engender such drastic domestic changes?

Against the conventional notion of the "lady" with her wifely duties and her "visiting and news," as Jane Austen put it, the Victorians created a powerful moral ideal for women. Some women were drawn to this ideal as a means of escape from the anemia of middle-class life, as George Eliot shows in her portrayal of Dorothea Brooke's high-minded ambition in *Middlemarch.* The best known "real-life" exponent of the ideal is of course Florence Nightingale, whose accomplishments as a nurse during the Crimean War strengthened the ideal of feminine self-sacrifice in the minds of women throughout England. Virginia Woolf's mother, Julia Stephen, and her half-sister Stella took pride in being remarkably able nurses who performed regular missions of mercy, visits to the workhouse, and vigils at sickbed, activities that the young Virginia participated in as well.[14] In an essay on domesticity, Julia Stephen wrote that "service is the condition of our being."[15] Jane Welsh Carlyle's letters as a young bride in remote Craigenputtock show a similarly fierce dedication as the guardian, nurse, and support of her husband. And there were many such lesser-known women who were stalwart wives, mothers, and standard-bearers in the community, as G. M. Young suggested in 1936 in *Victorian England: Portrait of an Age.* Young was born when Queen Victoria still had eighteen years to reign, and he cautioned his readers "how easy it is to misunderstand our grandmothers." The "most influential women" were reared to be "Custodians of the Standard," he wrote, and formidable presences they were.[16]

Born in 1846, Julia Stephen (upon whom the character of Mrs. Ramsey is based[17]) was of the generation Young refers to, the generation that imbibed *The Angel in the House* and "Of Queen's Gardens" and found in these works a high moral purpose for feminine existence. When Lily refers to the "astonishing power that Mrs. Ramsey had over one," how even her shadow was "full of authority," she alludes to Mrs. Ramsey's moral authority, to her developed "instinct" for good, her mysterious moral capacity "to rest in silence . . . in the extreme obscurity of human relationships."[18] Mrs. Ramsey never talks of her visits to the poor, for example; she merely sets out "punctually, directly. It was her instinct to go, an instinct like the swallows for the south . . . turning her infallibly to the human race, making her nest in its heart." (Woolf uses the same image for the deterioration of the house: "The swallows nested in the drawing-room.") Yet this instinct, Woolf continues, "was a little distressing to people who did not share it," people like Mr. Carmichael and Lily, who are inclined to believe in "the ineffectiveness of action, the supremacy of Thought."[19] Lily ultimately understands that her intellectual defense against Mrs. Ramsey's way of life is misguided when she admits that she cannot become "serious" about the society around her until she sees it through Mrs. Ramsey's eyes.[20] For Lily finally comes to *paint* in the morally inclusive way Mrs. Ramsey *lived.* In her painting, she makes of the moment "something permanent," as Mrs. Ramsey had been able to do in life. Although the painting "would be hung in the attic" and "destroyed," thinks Lily, "[W]hat did it matter?"[21] She has for a brief moment inhabited the unifying vision of her mentor, whose ghost visits her in the final scene, and who accomplishes the "vision" almost as much as Lily herself does.

Fifteen years after the publication of *To the Lighthouse,* Woolf delivered a paper entitled "Professions for Women" containing a more one-sided portrait of the Angel in the House. Reminiscing on her early days as a reviewer, she claims that it was the Angel "who used to come between me and my paper when I was writing reviews. It was she who bothered and wasted my time and so tormented me that at last I killed her. . . . The shadow of her wings fell on my page," urging the young Woolf to be feminine and "sympathetic" in her book reviews, and never to let "anybody guess that [she had] a mind of [her] own." With sinister determination, the domestic Angel "made as if to guide my pen." Whereas the shade of Mrs. Ramsey enables Lily to have her vision and complete her painting, in Woolf's lecture the Angel's shadow darkens her page, intent on disabling woman's creativity: "Had I not killed her she would have killed me. . . . Killing the Angel in the House was part of the occupation of the woman writer."[22] During the period in which Woolf composed *To the Lighthouse,* however, her ideological stance was less decided; she was able to honor the memory of the Victorian domestic woman and even to credit her with a creative power strong enough to guide the more modern woman's brush.

In the early reviews, Woolf wrestled with the notion that creating art was itself a form of living as valid as the continuation of family suggested at the conclusion of so many English novels. In reviewing E. M. Forster's *Aspects of the Novel,* she expresses impatience with his readiness to dismiss the claims of art as opposed to those of what he called "life." "What is this 'Life' that keeps on cropping up so mysteriously and so complacently in books about fiction? . . . Why is the pleasure that we get from the pattern in *The Golden Bowl* less valuable than the emotion which Trollope gives us when he describes a lady drinking tea in a parsonage? Surely the definition of life is too arbitrary, and requires to be expanded."[23] When she wrote *To the Lighthouse,* published in the same year as the review of Forster, Woolf was experiencing the early tremors of this expansion. For Lily's aesthetic vision is not independent or self-generating. It requires Mrs. Ramsey's vision and therefore leans on the "definition of life" that Woolf objects to in Forster. Entirely conscious of her own ambivalence, Woolf is bidding farewell to this older, more fecund definition of life, embodied by Mrs. Ramsey, who in turn is the fictive embodiment of the mother Woolf lost at the age of thirteen. "I have an idea," Woolf wrote while working on the novel, "that I will invent a new name for my books to supplant 'novel.' A new ———— by Virginia Woolf. But what? Elegy?"[24]

In being an elegy to the "angel in the house," *To the Lighthouse* is also an elegy to the house—or to the nineteenth-century domestic interior. In part 1, "The Window," the house acts as a frame for family life through which the world of things passes, and the interior is presented historically in terms of the passage of generations. In her bedroom Mrs. Ramsey invites her daughter to choose the piece of jewelry she will wear to dinner, as if Rose were choosing a jewel she herself might inherit, just as Mrs. Ramsey inherited her mother's sofa and her father's rocking chair, objects that furnish the interior. But like Minta Doyle's brooch, which Minta inherited from her grandmother and which is lost and left to decay unseen on the beach, the house and everything in it is destined for quiet dissolution. In part 2, "Time Passes," when the decay sets in, it becomes clear that the domestic happiness envisioned in part 1 was merely (merely!) a temporary protective cover or mortal disguise, like the shawl that covers the skull in the children's room. During the dinner party scene in part 1, Woolf describes the "mask-like look of faces seen by candlelight."[25] The faces appear as artistic renderings of themselves and the moment is made permanent—but it is only a moment. What do the lighted surfaces disguise but imminent decay?

After Mrs. McNab and Mrs. Bast temporarily reclaim the interior, the few remaining characters who come together in an act of commemoration are disoriented by a sense of loss: "the house, the place . . . all seemed strangers . . . as if the link that usually bound things together had been cut."[26] Mrs. Ramsey had imagined that Paul and Minta would carry on the domestic traditions that had been mysteriously sanctified the night of the dinner party: "this, and this, and this, she thought, going upstairs, laughing . . . at the sofa on the landing (her mother's); at the rocking-chair (her father's); at the map of the Hebrides. All that would be revived again in the lives of Paul and Minta . . . it was all one stream, and chairs, tables, maps, were hers, were theirs, it did not matter whose, and Paul and Minta would carry it on when she was dead."[27] But Mrs. Ramsey is wrong. Once she departs from the living, the domestic interior decays as assuredly as the dinner party dissolved when she left the room: "And directly she went a sort of disintegration set in."[28] The domestic ideal does survive in *To the Lighthouse,* but it survives in abstract form, in Mr. Ramsey's visionary, austere "kitchen table," in Lily's painting of Mrs. Ramsey, and in memory.

Even more emphatically than the interiors of earlier novelists, the interior in which the dinner party is set is associated with memory. Before the eight candles are lit—that incandescent moment when the characters suddenly come together in sympathy—Mrs. Ramsey remembers the drawing room of an old friend, whom she had known twenty years ago. She muses on the mysterious freshness of memory: "it fascinated her, as if, while she changed, that particular day, now become very still and beautiful, had remained there, all these years."[29] And as the scene draws to a close, she muses once again on the process by which events enter memory's domain: "With her foot on the threshold, she waited a moment longer in a scene which was vanishing even as she looked, and then, as she moved . . . and left the room, it changed, it shaped itself differently; it had become, she knew, giving one last look over her shoulder, already the past."[30] Mrs. Ramsey's dinner party will itself become a luminous memory to those present. Freud writes of how the memories that we retain are often representative of the particular "period of life" in which they take place, chosen over countless others because they epitomize a piece of time.[31] The dinner party represents Mrs. Ramsey's finest moment in making of the domestic "something permanent."

This is most strikingly shown when, just after the candles are lit, a "change at once went through them all, as if . . . they were all conscious of making a party together in a hollow, on an island." Like so many Robinson Crusoes maintaining a civilization in miniature—a dinner party is itself an emblem of the human refinement of animal function—they "had their common cause against the fluidity out there." The lighting of the candle is also a turning point in Crusoe's progress, the moment when, extending day into night, he can read at the end of a day's labor; and in Woolf's scene, the candlelight magically transforms objective reality, composing the faces "as they had not been in the twilight, into a party round a table."[32]

Even Crusoe's "earthenware pot" makes its appearance, an object that Woolf places in the foreground of her essay on Defoe's novel:

[*Robinson Crusoe*] is, we know, the story of a man who is thrown, after many perils and adventures, alone upon a desert island. The mere suggestion . . . is enough to rouse in us the expectation of some far land on the limits of the world; . . . of man, isolated from his kind, brooding alone upon the nature of society and the strange ways of men . . . We read; and we are rudely contradicted on every page. . . . [T]here is no solitude and no soul. There is, on the contrary, staring us full in the face nothing but a large earthenware pot.

To Woolf, Crusoe's earthenware pot symbolizes the "[r]eality, fact, substance" that dominate a narrative of "ruthless common-sense." God, Nature, even "Death does not exist. Nothing exists except the earthenware pot." Paradoxically, it is by means of this exclusive focus on the particular, Woolf insists, that Defoe achieves a sense of universal significance. At the conclusion of the essay, Woolf returns to the image of the earthenware pot, posing a question that she herself answers in the very scene in which she alludes to the pot in *To the Lighthouse:*

Thus Defoe, by reiterating that nothing but a plain earthenware pot stands in the foreground, persuades us to see remote islands and the solitudes of the human soul. By believing fixedly in the solidity of the pot and its earthiness, he has subdued every other element to his design; he has roped the whole universe into harmony. And is there any reason, we ask as we shut the book, why the perspective that a plain earthenware pot exacts should not satisfy us completely, once we grasp it, as man himself in all his sublimity standing against a background of broken mountains and tumbling oceans with stars flaming in the sky?[33]

In *To the Lighthouse* Mrs. Ramsey "peer[s] into the depths of the earthenware pot" as she muses on the "profound silence" of eternity: "Nothing need be said; nothing could be said. There it was, all round them. It partook, she felt, carefully helping Mr. Bankes to a specially tender piece, of eternity . . . there is a coherence in things, a stability; something, she meant, is immune from change and shines out (she glanced at the window with its ripple of reflected light) in the face of the flowing, the fleeting, the spectral."[34] Mrs. Ramsey grasps the perspective that "a plain earthenware pot exacts" and therefore offers those around her the "tender piece, of eternity" that defines the pleasurable domestic moment we witness. The prose itself "shines out" as well as in, registering at one moment the mysterious power of the lighted faces against the background of rippled, watery glass, then anchoring the scene with mundane discussions of food (English versus French cuisine, the skin of vegetables) and the inner thoughts of characters. Like a goddess, Mrs. Ramsey "put[s] a spell on them all," yet her family laughs at her when she discourses on "real butter and clean milk."[35] At the end of the scene, the poet-priest, Augustus Carmichael, rises in comic majesty, "holding his table napkin so that it looks like a long white robe," and "bow[s] to her as if he did her homage."[36] The earthenware pot, the "Neptune's banquet" dish of fruit, the priestly white napkin: these and other mundane objects take on sacred significance at the same time that their ephemeral nature is acknowledged. The "great brown dish" is consumed; the children grasp the pieces of fruit, destroying the aesthetic arrangement; the grandmother's brooch is lost forever.

Woolf's evocation of the fragile, transitory nature of domestic life intensifies in the second section of the novel, "Time Passes," in which the death of Mrs. Ramsey is followed by the deterioration of the house. The equation of Mrs. Ramsey's death with the decay of domesticity was perhaps overdetermined by the trauma Woolf experienced following the death of her mother, in which her grieving father proved incompetent to maintain the domestic stability his wife had provided.[37] Yet there are historical reasons for the equation as well, as suggested earlier. At the sensitive age of thirteen, Woolf experienced firsthand what was no doubt true of many middle-class homes of the period: that the stability of Victorian domesticity depended on the imagination, effort, and, above all, the culturally sanctioned moral authority of women like Julia Stephen, who were exclusively devoted to "the extreme obscurity of human relationships." As women's status changed, which it began radically to do in Julia Stephen's generation, such women gradually disappeared from the cultural scene.[38] The moral status that had been conferred on them rested on their exclusion from the public realm. Once they had the option of "earning their own living," as Woolf persistently puts it, the figure of the domestic angel as a "type" of all womanhood became obsolete, for her queenlike ascendancy within the private sphere hinged on the absence of other opportunities for women that might call into question the moral value of exclusive devotion to home and family. Mrs. Ramsey has no sense of any other path in life, for herself and for others—"people must marry; people must have children"[39]—and for that reason she lacks a sense of scale, as her habit of exaggeration proves. Victoria Rosner wittily analyzes the ways in which Mrs. Ramsey's conventional attitudes converge with her maintenance of the interior: "'windows open, doors shut'—'people must marry; people must have children.' . . . Does the house support Mrs. Ramsey's drive to reproduce the family, or does Mrs. Ramsey support the house's drive to remain intact and inhabited? Mrs. Ramsey's compulsion to propagate marriage is inseparable from her role as guardian of the domestic interior."[40] In "Time Passes," then, the changing domestic interior becomes the medium for something more human and particular than the elemental forces of "darkness" and "fluidity" that hasten its decay; it becomes the medium through which Woolf expresses not only the idea that "human character had changed," as she famously put it in another context,[41] but that a particular human type was vanishing from the cultural stage altogether.

Woolf was of the generation that produced that masterpiece of debunking, Lytton Strachey's *Eminent Victorians* (1918).

Proof of the tremendous sway that the image of self-sacrificing womanhood held over the imaginations of Victorians, the book includes among its chapters on powerful men of the establishment (Thomas Arnold, Cardinal Manning, General Gordon) a chapter on Florence Nightingale, whom Strachey describes as one possessed by a "Demon" will.[42] In marked contrast to her friend Strachey, Woolf does not dismantle the ideal represented by Mrs. Ramsey. Instead, she shows that for all of Mrs. Ramsey's limitations, what Mrs. Ramsey achieved was crucial to the community, for without her, the community nearly dissolves. In this respect, Woolf's elegy to her mother marks a departure from iconoclastic Bloomsbury and allies itself with a more reverent tradition that includes Matthew Arnold's poem to his father, "Rugby Chapel" (ca. 1860), and her contemporary Edmund Gosse's portrait of his father, Philip Gosse, in *Father and Son* (1907). Like Julia Stephen, Thomas Arnold and Philip Gosse had a magnanimous relation to members of the small communities they served. In Matthew Arnold's mind, his "[f]ervent, heroic, and good" father had the ability to keep those around him "combined";[43] and although Gosse's portrait of his father is divided (as is, to a lesser extent, Woolf's portrait of her mother), he allows us to witness the curious and compelling generosity of a man who, unlike his fastidious son, was capable of identifying with individuals radically different from himself, such as the Plymouth Brethren. What Woolf shares with these writers is the conviction that the Victorian parent being memorialized represents an extinct species. Like Arnold, Woolf suggests that the ideal embodied by her parent is no longer possible, yet, unlike Arnold and like Gosse, she has no interest in returning to it. Lily could never fill the shoes of Mrs. Ramsey, nor does she want to. At the end of *To the Lighthouse*, Lily stands outside the house, achieving her "vision" both because and in spite of Mrs. Ramsey's enduring presence.

The masterful ambivalence that Woolf registers in her "valediction,"[44] her farewell to Victorian domesticity, is writ large in the contrast between the concluding visions of domesticity in

To the Lighthouse and Forster's pre–World War I novel *Howards End*. Woolf knew the earlier novel well—Mrs. Bast is both ancestor and descendent of Forster's Leonard Bast—and she quite deliberately offers a less optimistic treatment of the future of domesticity. The clue to the difference between the novels in this respect rests on the characters of the two mothers, Mrs. Wilcox and Mrs. Ramsey. Both are quasi-mystical presences or domestic "angels," intelligent but not intellectual mothers, steady and unselfish givers to those around them, and intensely loyal wives. But while Mrs. Ramsey is a spirit *in* the house, Mrs. Wilcox is a spirit *of* it. "She seemed to belong not to the young people," writes Forster, "but to the house."[45] As Margaret says, "Houses are alive," and woe betide the individual who does not listen to what they can teach us.[46] As the novel's central symbol of continuity, Howards End resists the restless, "nomadic" lives of the characters, who move in and out of their houses, buying and selling real estate, transporting furniture from house to house, and all along generally declining until tragedy strikes at the end, that "help from the earth"[47] the old farmhouse affords.

The worst tragedy—separation of the loving sisters, Helen and Margaret Schlegel—never occurs because the house and the furniture restore their relationship. Once they are alone together at Howards End, they begin to talk about the familiar objects surrounding them that have been moved from Wickham Place, and with "each minute their talk became more natural."[48] The objects are filled with memories that unite them over all the divisions in their circumstances: Margaret's marriage to Henry, Helen's pregnancy, the innocent betrayals of each. Without a sense of place, individuals become strangers in Forster's novel, and it is by means of place that the antibourgeois utopia with which the novel ends is accomplished. In the final scene, we see Henry, Helen, and Margaret living peacefully together in a house that will be passed to Helen's illegitimate child. It is the house that binds them to one another, to England's agricultural past, and to the future. (Helen's child is descended, through Leonard Bast, from yeoman farmers.) Victoria Rosner sees in this conclusion "the emergence of a new kind of domestic interior," one that is provisional and experimental enough to enable "spontaneous life" for the inhabitants.[49] Consistent with the lives and work of the Bloomsbury artists, the characters take the home as "a kind of laboratory for social experimentation."[50] Yet, also like their Bloomsbury counterparts, they do not lead bourgeois lives; traditional family arrangements are no longer honored, and they live and work at home, as bourgeois workers are rarely able to do.

In the last section of *To the Lighthouse,* the house brings the characters together, but it does not unite them as it had done under Mrs. Ramsey's guardianship. In spite of Lily's triumphant "vision," Woolf registers a much deeper sense of communal loss than is communicated in Forster's novel. Conceived before the devastations of the war, Howards End is the spirit of England itself, the house and wych-elm tree "transcend{ing} any similes of sex"[51] as it endures through generations, world without end. In the final section of *To the Lighthouse,* the house is only temporarily saved from decay, and the characters stand outside and apart from one another, as if no one has the capacity to replace the unifying, humane presence of its former guardian. No character present in the final scene, to give one example, has the emotional intelligence to draw out the Mr. Tansleys of the world; Mr. Tansley himself is absent. Only in Mrs. Ramsey's presence are the intractable (Mr. Tansley) and the disaffected (Lily) able to let down their guard. Mr. Tansley is repellent to Lily, who can only tolerate him if she depends on Mrs. Ramsey's vision: "Her own idea of him was grotesque, Lily knew well, stirring the plantains with her brush. . . . He did for her instead of a whipping-boy. . . . If she wanted to be serious about him she had to help herself to Mrs. Ramsey's sayings, to look at him through her eyes."[52] Lily knows that she lacks Mrs. Ramsey's generous heart, a knowledge that is not changed by her recognition of the egotism and manipulativeness that occasionally attend Mrs. Ramsey's kindnesses. And while the spirit of private or domestic life is not lost in *To the Lighthouse*—as Rosner argues, Lily's modernist painting captures it[53]—Lily herself is standing outdoors when she paints it. A woman of the future, Lily is working outside the home.

With the emergence of middle-class women from the private realm, even in the relatively small numbers of the late nineteenth and early twentieth centuries, Victorian domesticity foundered. The Corbusian metaphor for the home—a "machine for living in"—now becomes the functional image for the bourgeois experience of home, the inevitable definition of home when both partners work outside of it. Without someone to care for the home and to mark it with welcoming human presence, it becomes a convenience, the necessary "machine for living in" for people who work. A machine does not need an angel to manage it; a machine merely needs servants to manage it, or more machines. Today, in spite of the proliferation of commodities promoting coziness, the bourgeois home is a machine full of machines, a setting for the accumulation of appliances designed to make domestic labor easier, faster, and cheaper for those who work.

Neither Forster nor Woolf imagines a future for bourgeois domesticity, and Woolf intimates that domesticity with a human face is doomed. When Lily asks Andrew what Mr. Ramsey's books are about, he replies: "'Subject and object and the nature of reality.' . . . And when she said Heavens, she had no notion what that meant. 'Think of a kitchen table then,' he told her, 'when you're not there.'"[54] With no one present to maintain the home, the domestic ideal survives only in abstract form, like the thousands of photographs of domestic interiors published yearly in "home magazines" in which human beings never figure. A prophetic wisdom haunts Woolf's portrait of the two old female servants who rehabilitate the interior of the Ramsey's house. For what remains of the bourgeois domesticity of the nineteenth century is either in the hands of paid domestic employees, who maintain the "machine for living in" and watch over children while parents and owners work, or housewives who do the work of maintaining the interior with none of the moral status of their predecessors. If the idea of the home as a "machine" repels us, we are more Victorian than we know. The power of our *memory* of Victorian domesticity is the subject of the next chapter.

Bourgeois Memory and Dream in the Domestic Interiors of Ingmar Bergman

There exists for each one of us an oneiric house, a house of dream-memory.
—Gaston Bachelard, *The Poetics of Space*

To move from the authors discussed in this book to the auteur Ingmar Bergman is to embrace a different medium, but one with a strong—some would argue inherent—literary component. Despite the various claims that have been made for a "pure cinema" since the subject was debated in Paris in the 1920s, mainstream or commercial films have always told stories, stories that were often derived from works of literature. This is especially true of Bergman's films. Throughout his career, Bergman has sought to incorporate in his images the inwardness that words, not limited by the materiality and specificity of the visual image, can evoke. And while Bergman has been faulted for "putting concepts into pictures" and eschewing a purely cinematic sequence of events,[1] the literary concepts that he developed in his films have often greatly enriched them. August Strindberg's influence on Bergman's films is arguably as important as that of early filmmakers like Victor Sjöström and Carl Dreyer. Bergman named Dickens as a "godfather" of *Fanny and Alexander,*[2] and it is difficult to imagine that he did not have Proust in mind when he was filming *Wild Strawberries.* As the bourgeois interior enters the world of memory and dream, moreover, we turn naturally to an artist whose own bourgeois past has so often gripped his imagination. Bergman is one of the most ardent readers of the domestic interior to follow the generation of James and Woolf.

Although few directors have given us deeper meditations on the bourgeoisie than Bergman has, few individuals seem to have been as determined to live a nonbourgeois existence as he. As of the publication of his autobiography in 1987, he had married five times, fathered eight children who remained with his wives, and gone into voluntary exile on the bleak island of Fårö in the Baltic Sea, as uncomfortably barren and therefore as nonbourgeois a setting as one is likely to find on the face of the earth. In *Persona* (1966), which was filmed on Fårö, the landscape appears to be without interior dimension, so exposed and open is its rugged terrain. Yet, as the son of a Lutheran minister growing up in Stockholm in the 1920s, Bergman had roots that reach back into the airless, overstuffed interiors of the late nineteenth-century bourgeoisie. A dialectical tension between open and closed spaces is felt across the Bergman oeuvre, yet its origins are perhaps as much a matter of Bergman's temperament as of his experience. As drawn to exploring extreme states of existence as Shakespeare was to the pun, Bergman was both metaphysician and artist. No sooner had he completed filming *Wild Strawberries,* which is about an old man on the brink of death, than he began filming *The Brink of Life,* a film about three women in a maternity ward. Yet Bergman's distinction as director of *Wild Strawberries* is less in the way he renders states of being that do not seem to refer to anything outside of themselves, absolute states of being such as dream-states, than in the way he shows how we move back and forth between these states and "reality." What is called reality is constantly being revised by memory and dream, and since Isak Borg's memories and dreams are often of domestic interiors, the domestic interior becomes a prime instrument of this process of revision.

In the earlier comparison between Vermeer's *The Love Letter* and the still from *Wild Strawberries,* I discuss the importance of framing to the idea of interiority. In *Wild Strawberries,* Bergman uses various framing devices—a framed photograph, a doorway, a car window—to explore the paradoxes of boundary and entry, restriction and possibility, that characterize Isak's spiritual journey. The framed photographs of the members of Isak's family that appear in the initial scene in his study are replaced by the *living* beings framed by the car window later in the film when the three youths awaken Isak from his slumber with song and flowers. These images act as markers, and in the dream-memory sequences that fall between them, Isak often stands at the edge of a frame, as if on a threshold. He gazes into a room that is a memory, a memory that takes the form of a room.

The identification of memories with particular spaces is an ancient one. When St. Augustine describes his memory as "an inner chamber" wherein "countless images" are "stored,"[3] he reveals the influence of the Greek view of memory, derived from the fifth-century poet Simonides, in which techniques of memorization are trained on spatial images. As Frances Yates has shown, these techniques led to the great memory theaters of Renaissance writers, who conceived of memory in concrete architectural terms.[4] The theory of memory on which the memory theaters were based suggests that our memories are situated in particular locations; they have a proximity to other memories that is associational, not logical, in nature.

Behind the imagination of the bourgeois interior as a memory space in *Wild Strawberries,* then, stands a long tradition of memory rooms in literature. Specifically bourgeois memory rooms predate Bergman as well, not only in *David Copperfield, Great Expectations,* and other novels discussed in these pages, but in a work Bergman also must have known, Proust's *Remembrance of Things Past.*[5] In the opening pages of *Swann's Way,* the narrator revisits the rooms of his childhood "in the long course of [his] waking dream":

Perhaps the immobility of the things that surround us is forced upon them by our conviction that they are themselves, and not anything else, and by the immobility of our conceptions of them. For it always happened that when I awoke like this, and my mind struggled in

an unsuccessful attempt to discover where I was, everything would be moving round me through the darkness:
things, places, years. . . . [My body's] memory, the com-
posite memory of its ribs, knees, and shoulder-blades, offered it a whole series of rooms in which I had at one time
or another slept.[6]

In *Wild Strawberries,* Isak's vision of his past commences in a
similar half-wakeful state in which the things around him lose
their "immobility" or grounding in the present. He has arrived
at his old summerhouse and is about to lie down under a tree,
but he sees a strawberry patch and exclaims, "Smultroonstäl-
let!" In Swedish *smultronställe* has both a literal and figurative
meaning: it refers both to the "special preserve" of each family
member, who lays claim to his own strawberry patch in late
June, and to a moment in the past that someone would like
to recapture.[7] As the camera cuts from the strawberry patch to
Isak's face, then to the summer house and back to his face again,
Isak's voiceover says, "Perhaps I was tired . . . How it happened
I don't know, but the clear reality of day gave way to the still
clearer images of memory which arose before my eyes with all
the force of reality." Suddenly, the house is transformed and
Isak is transported back to a summer morning in the 1890s.
His lovely cousin Sara, to whom he had been engaged in his
youth, appears before him. "Sara? Sara? It's your cousin Isak. I
have aged of course. But you haven't aged at all," says Isak, his
words driving to the heart of the bittersweet nature of memory.
In both Proust and Bergman, the search for lost time is a search
for lost space. As Diana Fuss writes of Proust's novel: "[T]ime
inhabits space; the one cannot be refound without the other."[8]

When Isak enters the house, the family is celebrating the
name day of Uncle Aron. All of Isak's long-dead brothers and
sisters are there, as well as his maternal aunt Olga, his deaf
Uncle Aron, and Sara. The parents and the young Isak are absent because they are fishing at the lake. In the sequence I have
already discussed in the introduction, Isak stands at the edge

of the frame, watching as the shades of his family celebrate, though it would be difficult to say who is haunting whom. Is the elderly Isak haunted by these memories of the past, or was he, as a boy, haunted by the lonely old man he would become? Does the past or the future hover over the present in this film? To recreate the palimpsest character of memory, Bergman superimposes Isak's present on his past, so that the "dead and resurrected" world of Isak's youth is framed in the perspective of his estrangement, and the man is always felt to be prefigured in the youth.[9]

As Philip and Kersti French have pointed out, Bergman drew on the romantic paintings of the Swedish painter Carl Larsson for these overexposed, shadowless interiors. Influenced by the arts and crafts movement in England, Larsson had a large impact on Swedish interior decoration and domestic architecture at the turn of the century, and Scandinavian audiences would have immediately recognized these interiors as images of the nation's past. Lit by the cinematographer Gunnar Fischer in the manner of Larsson, the furniture is identical to that found in Larsson's paintings, and the white suits and dresses cast no shadows.[10] The only shade is Isak himself, who hovers outside the doorframe, an image of modern European man dreaming of the past. The sequence also implies something like the reverse, however, in the way it portrays the disappearing world of the nineteenth century as already inhabited by the ghost of the future. As in Benjamin's phantasmagoric reading of nineteenth-century Paris in *The Arcades Project,* Bergman hints that the nineteenth century was already dreaming the dreams of the twentieth.

The world of Isak's past is that of late nineteenth-century bourgeois custom and ritual, as the formal meal, the name-day celebration, and the daily hoisting of the flag suggest. Proust writes of "those days . . . when one went to bed not because one felt inclined to but because it was bedtime, and signified one's willing acceptance of the complete rites of slumber."[11] What Proust calls the "anaesthetic effect of custom"[12] captures the essence of the kind of life the nineteenth-century bourgeois interior was created to foster. The *"interieur* forces the inhabitant to adopt the greatest possible number of habits," writes Benjamin, "habits that do more justice to the interior he is living in than to himself."[13] Aunt Olga, the mother-figure at the table, offers a steady stream of reprimands to keep the household in sync with these habits.

Wild Strawberries opens with another bourgeois interior, that of Isak's book-lined study in Stockholm, and we see both by the fastidious way he arranges objects on his desk and by the rituals imposed by his housekeeper that his life as an old man is also lived within the tight restrictions of habit. As the story unfolds, these habits and rituals are inextricably tied to Isak's professional dedication and to the strict solitude it has required of him. Our first image of him is from the back, as he stoops over his desk working, and we learn shortly that he is a doctor about to be honored at the university in Lund. In the voiceover, he tells us that he has withdrawn from "nearly all social intercourse." The camera moves slowly across the framed photographs in Isak's study as he speaks of the members of his family; the picture of his mother is placed next to a globe, for the mother is the "whole world" in this film, the one most responsible, besides Isak himself, for the sense of isolation that afflicts him. "More than film, a photograph stops time," writes Diana Fuss, offering a sense of fixity that "work[s] against the temporal flow of the cinema."[14] To insert a still photograph into a "moving picture," then, is to suggest the presence of a dramatic resistance to the film's narrative movement. In this way, the photographs of both Isak's mother and his wife suggest the problematic role each woman has played in his life.

As Isak leaves the study, he is momentarily distracted by the sight of a chess game he is playing with himself, a telling image of his intellectual self-absorption. Most telling of all, however, is the presence of a dog whose hanging teats show that she has nursed puppies—the second image of a mother in the quietly powerful scene. Isak kindly beckons to the dog, who follows him obediently out of the room, suggesting the disciplined animality to which libidinal pleasure has been subordinated in Isak's orderly, civilized universe. Isak is as "kind" to the dog as he was to his wife, as the wife's despairing narration later in the film suggests, when she recounts his condescending forgiveness of her adultery. In the space of a few minutes, Victor Sjöstrom, under Bergman's direction, has established the character traits that the film will plumb: the loneliness that has disfigured Isak's soul, the gentleness that disguises condescension, and the sorrow that hides more sorrow. As Oscar Wilde wrote, behind joy there may be many things, but "behind sorrow there is always sorrow"[15]—a phrase that gives us an accurate description of Isak's ravaged face.

When Isak decides to change his plans for the day and drive instead of fly to Lund, the outrage of Miss Agda, his housekeeper, suggests how rare such expressions of spontaneity are in his life. Yet this small act of spontaneity results in blessings both for himself and his son Evald. His impulsiveness prompts his daughter-in-law to her own spur-of-the-moment decision to return with him to her husband in Lund. And so Isak returns Evald's estranged wife to him; and, in revisiting his own past, which he does on the road trip, he is able to prepare for what the previous night's dream has told him he must do: to give up life, "choose death, and make friends with the necessity of dying," as Freud wrote of another difficult old man.[16]

In the image of Isak on page 9 and in others in the sequence, the life upon which he gazes, the idealized Victorian past, literally marginalizes his being, and the story that unfolds reveals the terrible extent of his estrangement. The Frenches point out that the other artist alluded to in one of these images besides Larsson is Edvard Munch, in whose *Jealousy* (1895) a similarly distraught male figure "looking both straight ahead and into himself" stands to the right of the canvas while, in the background, a naked woman plucks an apple for a man beside her. "In *Wild Strawberries* this account of the Fall is replaced by an Edenic scene from Larsson."[17] The Fall, of course, does arrive later, when Isak is forced to revisit the scene of his wife's adultery in a garden. Bergman's debt to Freud is evident once again in this scene, which was originally intended to include snakes on the ground. The ethical idealism of the professional Isak, who as a young man was too ashamed to enjoy kissing Sara, has consisted in the progressive renunciation of instinct. The animality of libidinal desire, already hinted at by the dog, is made clear in the garden scene, in which a boorish man copulates with his wife. No middle ground between the repression of desire and its barbaric satisfaction appears to be possible for the young Isak. He and his generation are cursed by what Freud called "the fateful development of civilization."[18]

Before the garden-adultery scene transpires in Isak's dream, he visits another bourgeois interior, that of his mother. The house of Mrs. Borg is full of disturbing relics of the past: the faceless watch that suggests the failed legacy of his father, the photograph of Isak and his brother as children that his mother dismisses as "rubbish," and the doll that Marianne holds in her arms as a symbol of her own childlessness. Like the mysterious clock, which had appeared earlier in Isak's nightmare, these objects, or what they represent, must be reanimated or given life. What Bergman calls Isak's "emotional frigidity" has in a sense stopped time by freezing the development of his love for his son; his daughter-in-law's childlessness is a result of this sterile legacy. Marianne stands before the mother "and sees the connection," said Bergman, "the icy chain of aggressions and boredom."[19] But change can take place only after Isak reenters his past a second time in the dream he experiences while asleep in the car. There he gazes into yet another bourgeois interior, in which he sees Sara and Sigfrid, dressed as his parents might have dressed in an earlier period, enjoying the idyllic formalities of bourgeois marriage. Sigfrid kisses Sara on the back of the neck as she plays the piano, then on the lips. They sit down together to enjoy a meal and simultaneously sip from glasses of wine in the candlelight. In stark contrast to the adultery scene, which is soon to follow, eros and civilization are ideally blended in this slow, dancelike, luminous portrait of bourgeois life, and once again, Isak is excluded from it. The love of both his mother and Sara is denied him, and his humiliation is registered when, desperate in his voyeurism to look through the window, he grasps a nail on the wall and pierces his hand, giving him the stigmata that suggests his pain as well as "the possibility of salvation."[20]

In my discussion here I have neglected the religious and philosophical dimensions of the film, about which much has already been written, in order to draw attention to one of the film's primary strengths: its evocation of the relations between generations by means of the mise-en-scène of its domestic interiors. As Robin Wood writes, "Bergman encompasses five generations within the twenty-four hour unity of the film"[21] when he has Isak's mother talk of her mother and Marianne express her fears for the child she is carrying. Interiors are used to symbolize the three generations of Isak, his mother, and his son. In Evald's house in Lund, the last interior we see, Bergman repeats the richly suggestive image of Isak standing at a threshold, looking through a doorway, but in this instance, instead of suggesting Isak's exclusion, the image suggests his participation. ("I am the door," says Jesus.[22]) He and Miss Agda watch together as Evald and Marianne begin their reconciliation, a reconciliation that Isak himself has made possible. All the interiors of *Wild Strawberries* have acted as way stations to this one. Whereas Isak's study is furnished in the same late-Victorian style and lit in the same muted tones as his mother's house, the airiness of the space in Evald's house links it to the bright vision of Isak's waking dream of his former summerhouse.

This is not to suggest that, by means of the doorway image alone, we expect the future of Evald and Marianne to be idyllically happy—the family legacy and the uncertain mores of modern life will make that impossible—but something has been achieved. Like Cinderella, Marianne reclaims her slippers when she returns to the house later in the evening before going to the dance, and in a film in which so much has been lost, this is a positive sign. The suggestion of Christian baptism or regeneration that follows this scene, when Isak, reentering the dreamlike world of water, wind, and sun of his childhood, watches as one of his siblings falls into the water and is thrown a life preserver, is more powerful than the image of Marianne finding and showing her slippers to Isak, but without the small thematic details to support the larger ones, *Wild Strawberries* wouldn't be what it is. "The great things of life are what they seem to be, and for that reason . . . are often difficult to interpret," writes Oscar Wilde. "But the little things in life are symbols."[23] Whenever Bergman tries to articulate the "great things of life" directly, the film falls flat; most viewers do not know how to interpret Evald's statement of despair in the coastal scene that Marianne narrates to Isak in the car, for example, because he speaks the textbook existentialism of the fifties, the decade in which the film was made. But Marianne's finding her slipper is one of those "little things" whose symbolic meaning breaks the heart.

In *Cries and Whispers* (1972), no such redemption is to be found in bourgeois life. Taking place in nineteenth-century interiors steeped in the red of human blood—the color of "the interior of the human soul," according to Bergman[24], the story opens with images of terrible suffering: Agnes, played by Harriet Andersson, her face contorted with pain, is suffering the final stage of terminal cancer. "It is early morning and I am in pain," she writes in her diary. "My sisters are taking turns staying up"—but we have already seen that her sisters are sleeping soundly. Bergman seems intent on showing that in habitually denying the reality of death, bourgeois daily life itself had become a living death. In the words of Benjamin: "In these rooms, death was not provided for. That is why they appear so cozy by day and become the scene of bad dreams at night."[25] The most frightening sequences in the film are taken up with these death-dreams; Bergman's aim, he said, was to give "Death . . . its voice."[26]

The only person who is able to cope with death is the Tolstoian figure of the servant, Anna, played by Kari Sylwan. Reminiscent of Gerasim in *The Death of Ivan Ilych,* Anna watches over her mistress's body and spirit just as she keeps up the domestic interior. As in *Wild Strawberries* and *Fanny and Alexander,* the figure of the domestic servant is as essential to the maintenance of the interior as to the bodies and souls of its inhabitants, as if Bergman were suggesting that all aspects of bourgeois existence—except the measureless suffering of the bourgeois individual—owe their continuance to class relations.

At the opposite extreme from the partitioned, solid, and defined spaces of *Wild Strawberries* and *Cries and Whispers* are the porous and permeable spaces of the interiors of *Persona,* which appeared in 1966. Whereas rooms in *Wild Strawberries* announce Isak's separation from others, the rooms in *Persona* imply the blending of personalities. When Liv Ullman enters Bibi Anderson's room on a foggy night, she passes through a sheer lace curtain, as if to suggest the frail partition between their psyches. If in *Wild Strawberries* domestic barriers create neurosis, in *Persona* their absence creates psychosis.

Bergman solved this no-exit psychology of space in *Fanny and Alexander* when he adopted a more affirmative view of the bourgeoisie. Here the stylized, monochromatic interiors of *Cries and Whispers* give way to far more vital images, and the bourgeois interior is reclaimed as the refuge and theater of the imaginative life of the child, a mimetic *spielraum* or space for play in the profoundest sense. The film pays tribute both to what the interior gave to Bergman as a filmmaker, as the persistent image of the magic lantern shows, and to what it gave the children of his era: a small universe of colors, objects, and sounds, a "world of matter,"[27] as Benjamin puts it, safely enclosed in one of custom and ritual. The film opens on December 24, 1907, on the eve of the forty-third Christmas celebration in Helena Ekdahl's house. Helena's grandson Alexander, played by Bertil Guve, is gazing dreamily at a little nativity scene produced by a magic lantern. He calls out the names of his sister, mother, father, and servant. He wanders through the silent, richly furnished rooms, passing from his parents' quarters into those of his grandmother. He hides in his grandmother's bed, stands by the window gazing at his hand through the lace curtain, and then hides again under a table. Looking drowsily out from his hiding place, he gazes at a nude statue of a woman on the left of the frame as it magically raises its arm. A maid enters the frame on the right and lifts her arm in a similar gesture as she pours coals into a stove. For the child, the mundane is transformed. (See opposite.)

The "prerogative of the child," writes Bergman, "is to move in complete freedom between magic and oatmeal porridge"[28]— for the child practices the primitive form of worship discussed in the last chapter, the faith of the fetish. In *Fanny and Alexander,* the incandescent object-worship of the child is sovereign over the fetishisms of the adults in the film, the sexually perverse and commodity fetishisms identified by Freud and Marx. (These fetishisms are nicely epitomized in a single image: the paper "contract" that Gustav Ekdahl dashes off for the domestic servant Maja in which he promises to make her proprietress of a coffee shop. The contract suggests the commodification of their lovemaking at the same time that the gouty Gustav uses it to delay consummation.) Bergman's aim in *Fanny and Alexander* is to reassert the imagination and faith of the child over the corruption and misery of the adult: "I want to depict, finally, the joy that I carry with me in spite of everything, and which I so seldom and so feebly have given attention to in my work."[29]

Bergman's prologue to the screenplay of *Fanny and Alexander* makes clear what the film hints at visually: that the Ekdahl interior is a palimpsest, a place where the present is written over the past, the past over the present. The apartment is inhabited by two generations of Ekdahls, each of whom resides in a differently styled interior. In the grandmother's darker rooms, the furnishings are late Victorian, whereas Alexander's

In a publicity still from Bergman's *Fanny and Alexander* (1982), the bourgeois family is seated in the bourgeois interior. When at the beginning of the film Alexander gazes into this space, emptied of people, the statue on the left comes alive. (Courtesy of the Svensk Filmindustri and the Swedish Film Institute)

parents' quarters are decorated in a brighter, more modern and eclectic taste with art nouveau touches. Bergman writes that it is Alexander "who in a reckless moment venture[s] to open the door between the two apartments," passing from the present space of his parents into his grandmother's older world.[30] The child of the bourgeois interior inhabits different levels of time, so it is appropriate that it is the child who can see the ghost that others cannot see.

In *Berlin Childhood around 1900* (composed in the early 1930s and revised in 1938 but not published in his lifetime), Walter Benjamin pays tribute to the bourgeois household of his childhood in much the same way as Bergman by invoking the magic potential that domestic objects possess for the child. Likewise indebted to Proust, Benjamin cites some of the same objects and rituals of late nineteenth-century bourgeois life that Bergman memorializes: the lighting of the gas lamps

on the street, the coal-burning stoves, the massive and lush
Victorian furnishings, and the secular mysteries of Christmas.
In a section entitled "Hiding Places" he writes:

> I already knew all the hiding places in the house, and
> would return to them as to a home ground where every-
> thing is sure to be in its familiar place. My heart would
> pound. I held my breath. Here I was enveloped in the
> world of matter. It became monstrously distinct for me,
> loomed speechlessly near. In much the same way, a man
> who is being hanged first comes to know what rope and
> wood are. The child who stands behind the doorway cur-
> tain himself becomes something white that flutters, a
> ghost. The dining table under which he has crawled turns
> him into the wooden idol of the temple; its carved legs
> are four pillars. And behind a door, he is himself the door,
> is decked out in it like a weighty mask and, as sorcerer,
> will cast a spell on all who enter unawares. Not for a fairy
> kingdom would he be found. . . . the house was an arsenal
> of masks.[31]

For the child, the objects of the interior are animated, and he
himself takes on magical powers. He becomes the door, his figure engraved on it as on a talisman. In the act of returning to
his hiding places "as to a home," the spirit of the child merges
with a world that would otherwise confront him with an in-
timidating exteriority: the world of inert "matter," of massive
Victorian furniture. The essential paradox of bourgeois domestic space that Benjamin and Bergman explore is that of the
interior as both *mask* and *inwardness,* both surface and depth.
As Howard Eiland writes:

> The child is collector, flaneur, and allegorist in one. He
> lives in an antiquity of the everyday: for him, everything
> is natural and therefore endowed with chthonic force. His
> relation to things is wholly mimetic. That is, he enters
> with all his senses into the world of things . . . and masks

himself with [them], above all with pieces of furniture in his household, seeing from out of their midst. The world for him is an "arsenal of masks." Everything is alive, full of eyes and ears, as in the animistic world of fairy tales. Just as a spinning wheel, slipper, or mirror sets up a force field in the tale, drawing characters and events into a pattern, so the child is initiated into the secret life of ordinary objects, often the most minuscule. He picks up indecipherable signs from the rattling of the rolled-up window blinds or the rustling of the branches that brush up against the house. . . . The child builds his nest in the depth of the everyday, secure and hidden (*geborgen*) in the fragile magic of the "home."[32]

Benjamin alludes to "the almost immemorial feeling of bourgeois security" that emanated from this magical space. The type of furniture, he suggests, "having capriciously incorporated styles of ornament from different centuries, was thoroughly imbued with itself and its own duration. Poverty could have no place in these rooms, where death itself had none."[33] The "arsenal of masks," then, serves to ward off death; and the wealth of the bourgeois household makes total immersion in a seemingly timeless world of objects and ritual possible. When Alexander is moved to the sparely furnished house of the bishop, he loses his ability to hide and to dream.

From the beginning of the film, with the magic lantern's projection of the nativity scene, the worlds of theater and formal religion are directly linked, yet each is finally encompassed by the world of the bourgeoisie. The sensualist Gustav Ekdahl, who owns a lavish restaurant, stands at the center of this world. What joins images of the theater to those of the church is not simply the idea of performance and ritual but that which performance and ritual disguise and repress: violence and death. After the children are rescued and returned to the puppet-filled shop of the Jewish antique dealer and moneylender, Alexander's frightening encounter with the androgynous Ishmael is crosscut with the conflagration at the bishop's house. Beneath theatrical illusion lies the oedipal hatred Ishmael urges Alexander to express, just as beneath the bishop's religion sadism rages. In presenting these violent associations Bergman is of course far more indulgent of the theater, and all that is connected with it, than of the church. From the beginning of the film, the Jewish antique dealer, proprietor of theatrical props and former lover of the actress Mrs. Ekdahl, has a special relation to objects in the bourgeois interior, one that suggests mastery of their aesthetic, economic, and magical power. He gives jewelry to Mrs. Ekdahl and uses one of his antique chests to spirit the children away from the bishop's house. As in James's *The Golden Bowl,* the Jew in *Fanny and Alexander* plays a pivotal role in the manipulation of objects that prove critical to the plot, though Bergman's more positive view of the Jew, as sorcerer, lover, and good father, is also richer and more elaborate.[34]

The film ends by affirming the generous, tolerant world of the bourgeoisie, one of sensuality and procreation, in full view of its class interests, money values, and neuroses, which Bergman unfailingly yet affectionately portrays. The dazzling final celebration, led by Gustav, makes this clear. "It is not at all shameful to take pleasure in the little world" or to delight in the "tangible yet immeasurable" capacity of human beings, declares Gustav as he gazes on the newborn children. Although the film concludes with the sudden, ghoulish reappearance of the bishop as the Hamletian ghost of Alexander's father murdered—the stepfather's ghost has replaced the real father's ghost—the lurking fear of ghostly apparitions in the nineteenth-century bourgeois interior is only "the price . . . paid for security." Because in these rooms, "death was not provided for," death is forever lurking.[35]

In Bergman's modern interiors, such as Evald's house in *Wild Strawberries* or the tightly framed interiors in *Scenes from a Marriage* (1973), the problem is not what is lurking but what is missing. This is why Marianne's finding of her slippers is so touching; it signals the reclamation of something that was absent: love between husband and wife. In the interiors imagined by W. G. Sebald, subject of my last chapter, the question posed is also one of absence—absence not in the sense of emptiness but in the paradoxical fullness of what has been forgotten. In *Austerlitz,* the narrator muses on "how everything is constantly lapsing into oblivion with every extinguished life, how the world is, as it were, draining itself, in that the history of countless places and objects which themselves have no power of memory is never heard, never described or passed on."[36] In Sebald's works, dreams do not begin in memory but in its failure, and the aura of objects is never meditated without acknowledging the paradoxical absence of the human. Bergman is still part of the world of Proust and Dickens, in which objects retain their radiant, talismanic power. The unnerving capacity of these objects and the interiors that contain them to provide a battleground for the soul reassures us that a soul exists. And no one needs this reassurance more than the bourgeois.

Conclusion: John Updike, W. G. Sebald, and the Afterlife of the Bourgeoisie

Yet one of the oddities of our life as it rushes past is that we are so eager in our work, so avid for pleasure, that we are seldom able to treasure and hold fast the given particularities of the moment. And so, even at an advanced age, we still have a duty to acknowledge the human—which never leaves us—in its singularities.

—Goethe, Letter to Moritz Seebeck (1832)

In the course of writing this book, I was frequently reminded of a passage in *German Men and Women,* Walter Benjamin's edition of letters written by "the great exemplars" of the preindustrial German middle class.[1] In this collection, Benjamin pays homage to the spirit of an earlier bourgeoisie, one that existed before "wealth and speed [became] what the world admires."[2] The letters reach deeply into daily life in their references to the weather, to family, and to the domestic interior. Commenting on a letter written by a visitor to Immanuel Kant's dwelling in Königsberg, Benjamin points to the unpretentiousness of the interior and suggests that "the human" is contingent on certain "conditions and limits": "Conditions and limits of humanity? Certainly. . . . [W]henever there is talk of humanity, we should not forget the narrowness of the middle-class room into which the Enlightenment shone." Throughout *German Men and Women,* Benjamin stresses the "interdependence" of the more modest interiors of an earlier age and "true humanity," implying that one of the forces to destroy the humane spirit of this class was the immense prosperity brought by industry.[3] Benjamin's use of the word *human* in this context may come from Goethe's letter to Moritz Seebeck, a quote from which serves as the epigraph to this chapter.[4]

It comes as no surprise that in reflecting on the Enlightenment from the perspective of Europe in the first decades of the twentieth century, a period in which the status of the human had been called into question, Benjamin should look for signs of humanity in an earlier era of German history. What is surprising is that he locates these signs in the domestic interior. Benjamin's analyses of the phantasmagoric interiors of the nineteenth century suggest that he understood them to represent a kind of "afterlife" to the more vital spaces of the past. In his image of the Victorian dwelling as a "receptacle for the person," for example, he imagines the residence as a kind of coffin, enfolding the dweller in a cushioned space that resembles the inside of a velvet-lined compass case.

Another "afterlife" occurs at the beginning of the twentieth century, when modern architecture renders obsolete the already moribund humanity of the nineteenth-century interior, and the signs of embedded human presence seem to disappear altogether. In the modernist interiors of Le Corbusier, constructed with materials like steel and glass on which it is impossible to leave a human imprint, all trace of the human is left behind. An "afterlife" implies a past, however, and from its earliest appearance in fiction, the bourgeois interior has always registered and sought to compensate for the loss of a more secure state. Coming after authors who for nearly three centuries have examined the homesickness inherent in the experience of home, the contemporary writers I shall consider here are fully conscious of their inheritance.

Both John Updike's "The Afterlife" (1994) and W. G. Sebald's "Dr Henry Selwyn" (1997) are set in English country houses inhabited by characters who have left their country of origin to settle in the county of Norfolk. "Flinty Dell" is the name given to Updike's house by its American inhabitants, and Sebald's residence is called "Prior's Gate." A dell is a secluded place or haven, and "Prior's Gate" suggests entrance into an earlier life. Both associations are familiar to bourgeois dwellings I have considered thus far. A *flinty* dell further hints at the nature of most bourgeois havens: they are never as comfortable as we imagine them to be. The main character in "The Afterlife," Carter Billings, suffers an accident in the interior of Flinty Dell, and in Sebald's story, Dr. Selwyn has removed himself from the great house at Prior's Gate, preferring to live in a smaller dwelling on the grounds of the estate.

Both Selwyn and Billings are older men experiencing life after their prime. Each meditates on the past and half-consciously dwells on the future—on the conundrum of life continuing beyond his own death. The idea of an "afterlife" figures in each author's imagination of class as well, in that the bourgeois class the characters once knew is a thing of the past. In neither story are we given the sense of a future generation, and the characters appear to be living in a kind of limbic or "weightless" afterstate, conscious of the "cosmic joke just beneath mundane appearances."[5] Dr. Selwyn is first seen lying motionless in his garden, "his head propped on his arm . . . altogether absorbed in contemplation of the patch of earth immediately before his eyes."[6] Carter Billings holds bits of flint in his hand, meditating their mysterious durability. ("They were porous, pale, intricate, everlasting."[7]) While the philosophical and moral texture of each work expresses a specific European or American historical perspective, in both stories the authors draw on the tradition of English fiction to make highly self-conscious contributions of their own to the long-established image of the bourgeois interior.

Flinty Dell

Born in 1932, Updike came of age in the 1950s, in what one critic identifies as "the final decade of the industrial age." As power shifted from the bourgeois owners of the means of production to the technocrats and bureaucrats who would direct the process of technological innovation and economic growth, the bourgeoisie declined in social significance. The

1950s have also been described as the last period in which the American middle classes were loosely held together by a uniform set of values emanating from what is called the "Protestant Establishment."[8] Updike's vision of suburban bourgeois life is imbued with a kind of comic Calvinist fervor in that his characters sin vigorously, but their "faith"—the faith their "creator" has placed in them—is greater. In the main phase of Updike's creativity, the suburbs are like a fallen Eden in which transgression is as much a part of middle-class life as obedience to convention. When Piet Hanema, the adulterous hero of *Couples* (1968), escapes detection by wriggling out of a bathroom window, he comes upon another adulterous couple necking in the grass. They tell him: "[Y]ou may tell one person . . . those are the rules," and in exchange, they may tell another couple about Piet's jumping.[9] At the end of the novel, Piet, divorced and with a new wife, begins a new cycle in another suburb as "another couple."

This sense of a community is no longer felt in Updike's later collection of stories, *The Afterlife.* The title story begins: "The Billingses, so settled in their ways, found in their fifties that their friends were doing sudden, surprising things." One friend runs off with a Jamaican physical therapist while his wife takes a woman lover and eventually turns their suburban house into a lesbian commune. Another friend is revealed to have embezzled millions from his brokerage firm and is sent to prison. "And then the Billingses' very dearest friends, Frank and Lucy Eggleston, upped and moved to England. It was something, Frank confided, they had thought about for years; they detested America, the way it was going—the vulgarity, the beggary, the violence."[10]

No longer the garden-variety adultery of Updike's earlier fiction, which had stimulated as much as violated the sense of community in his novels, these transgressions mark a radical overturning of bourgeois racial, sexual, and legal norms, the devolution of suburbia itself. Taking the conservative slogan of the Vietnam era literally—"America: Love it or leave it"—the Egglestons have abandoned America altogether to embrace the bourgeois traditions of a bygone era. They purchase an antique house in Norfolk, join the local church, adopt local customs and speech idioms, and forget about the community and country they once knew. Lucy Eggleston takes up "village good works" even though, as she observes, the socialist system provides for people: "They're taken care of, you see, and compared with their fathers and grandfathers aren't so badly off. The *cruelty* of the old system of hired agricultural labor is almost beyond imagining; they worked people absolutely to death."[11] A reactionary in America, Lucy has become a nineteenth-century liberal in England.

The desire to return to a more protected bourgeois state is, as we have seen, part and parcel of bourgeois consciousness going back to Defoe. The Egglestons give their house a name that is reminiscent of Dickens's Dingley Dell, which itself nostalgically recalled the earlier dwellings of the preindustrial bourgeoisie. ("Veels vithin veels," as Sam Weller says to Pickwick.[12]) Yet in spite of the irony directed at the Egglestons, Updike's main character knows that he too cannot let go of the bourgeois values of the past. Carter feels "the charm of the timeless" at Flinty Dell and, shopping in a nearby village, he impulsively makes a purchase for his house, "as if one more piece of furniture might keep [his wife] at home,"[13] away from the social work Lucy's talk about village charities is encouraging. That the essential bourgeois myth is still accessible to Carter is again shown in the central symbolic event of the story: the accident Carter suffers on the first night of his arrival.

Carter's disastrous trip to the bathroom on a moonless night is reminiscent of Pickwick's getting lost in the dark corridor of the inn at Ipswich. The uncanny appearance of objects in the night, the treacherous staircase, the confusing succession of doors, and, above all, the comic disorientation of the hero, all bring Pickwick's adventure to mind:

In the night, Carter awoke and needed to go to the bathroom. All that port. A wind was blowing outside. Vague black-on-blue tree shapes were thrashing. Not turning on a light, so as not to wake Jane, he found the bedroom door, opened it softly in the dark, and took two firm steps down the hall toward where he remembered the bathroom was. On his second step, there was nothing but air beneath his foot. His sleepy brain was jolted into action; he realized he was falling down the stairs. As he soared through black space, he had time to think what a terrible noise his crashing body would make. . . . Then something—some*one,* he felt—hit him in a solid blow in the exact center of his chest, right on the sternum, and Carter was standing upright on what seemed to be a landing partway down the stairs. . . . [E]merging again into the dark hall, he couldn't find the way back to his bedroom. Walls as in a funhouse surrounded him. A large smooth plane held a shadowy man who actually touched him, with an abrupt oily touch, and he realized it was himself, reflected in a mirror. On the three other sides of him there were opaque surfaces paneled like doors. Then one of the doors developed a crack of dim blue light and seemed to slide diagonally away; Carter's eyes were adjusted to the dark enough to register wallpaper—faintly abrasive and warm to his touch—and the shiny straight gleam, as of a railroad track, of the banister. He reversed his direction. There seemed many doors along the hall, but the one he pushed open did indeed reveal his bedroom. The wind was muttering, fidgeting at the stout English window sash, and as Carter drew closer to the bed he could hear Jane breathe. He crept in beside her and in the same motion fell asleep.[14]

For all the staidness of the Egglestons, their domestic interior is a dynamic space. Objects are alive, having their fun with Carter Billings. The wind mutters and fidgets at the window sash like Catherine Earnshaw's ghost, while the bourgeois man within encounters himself in the mirror as the "shadowy" one-dimensional figure he fears he is. Later in the story, as Carter becomes increasingly conscious of and elated by a sense of the precariousness of each moment, he deliberates: "He felt he had been useful enough, in his life, and had seen enough people."[15] Like Dr. Selwyn, Carter is at last imagining his existence as an end in itself, as divine a fact as a bit of flint, and not as a means to an end determined by others.

The domestic interior is what makes this epiphany possible, for it is where Carter first "reverse[s] his direction," realizes he has been spared, and reconsiders the world around him. "Next morning, as he examined the site of his adventure, he marveled that he had not been killed. . . . He had no memory of grabbing anything, or of righting himself. But how had he regained his feet? Either his memory had a gap or he had been knocked bolt upright. If the latter, it seemed a miracle."[16] Full of gratitude, he now looks at the world with fresh eyes. In an excursion with Lucy and his wife the next day, the near-misses continue to work their magic. He drives under a tree that crashes a few minutes later. Birdwatching, he is mysteriously impelled to look behind him one more time in search of a heron: "And there [it] was . . . motionless within the wind, standing in midair with his six-foot wingspread—an angel."[17] His car is "gently rocked in the wind, as if being nudged by a giant hand," and, caressing his chest, he remembers the blow in the night, "his passport to this day like no other," as if it were "a father's rough impatient saving blow."

While nothing in life is safe, Updike suggests, *this* bourgeois is clearly in God's hand. America may be falling apart and Carter himself is nearly killed, yet he is nonetheless secure. Nearing the end of his career, Updike renews his faith in the safety of the soul of the bourgeois. At the conclusion of the story, a touching reference to a new dawn is made when Carter notices a bit of paint—"an azure fleck of today's dawn"—in the little fingernail of his host, who has risen early to catch the morning light in a painting. Even though "The Afterlife" is as saturated with a sense of impending death as the rain-soaked landscape is "dyed . . . in an ink that rolled across the pale speckled fields"[18]—nature and art repeatedly merge in Updike's images—the story is essentially a comedy in which the bourgeois interior is a funhouse full of peril. Like many a pilgrim before him, Carter Billings must find his way in the dark, and with wise wit, Updike sets his perilous journey in the interior of a house that is as much myth as reality.

Not all of the interiors in *The Afterlife* are as buoyant as that of Flinty Dell. "The Brown Chest" is a Proustian study of a domestic object that contains family relics like lace tablecloths, college diplomas, and "still brown pictures" of dead people. "The chest went down and down, into the past," writes Updike, communicating an oppressive sense of both accumulation and loss. In "The Black Room," with its echoes of Poe and Charlotte Perkins Gilman's "The Yellow Wallpaper," the domestic interior is associated with terror. The "sad spirits from long ago locked into events that couldn't change"[19] haunt houses in several stories in Updike's collection. But in the title story these spirits, like playful poltergeists, restore the character who encounters them to life, "righting" his fall.

Dr. Henry Selwyn's Hermitage

If Carter Billings is heir to the more comic and redemptive traits of bourgeois individualism, in Dr. Henry Selwyn, we see the full development of the bourgeois isolation of Robinson Crusoe. Dr. Selwyn has abandoned the country of his youth and anglicized his name. After leading a life of ambition and adventure, he takes up residence in a remote stone dwelling "furnished with the essentials," his "only companions [being] plants and animals."[20] Like Robinson Crusoe, Dr. Selwyn occupies the dwelling of a survivor and lives only on food he grows himself. But whereas Defoe's character is symbolically engaged in building a culture, England after the Glorious Revolution of 1688, Dr. Selwyn has outlived one, the culture of prewar Europe. Sebald's narrator is acutely aware of the effects of time: "Nature itself was groaning and collapsing beneath the burden we placed on it."[21] (No uplifting harmony of nature and art here.) The violence and waste of history are palpable yet unspoken presences in Sebald's story until its ending, when Dr. Selwyn takes his own life "with a bullet from his heavy hunting rifle."[22] We may recall that Robinson Crusoe had fired "the first Gun that had been fir'd [on the island] since the Creation of the World" as if in celebration of the invention of gunpowder.

All of the essential ingredients of bourgeois dwelling enumerated at the opening of my chapter on *Robinson Crusoe* are present in Sebald's story in highly ironic form: the image of the home as fortress (a small stone dwelling or "hermitage" is Dr. Selwyn's last refuge); the association between the home and private ownership (he has abandoned the main residence, which he considers to be the property of his wife, and resides in a humbler dwelling on the estate); the role of domestic arts in the home (he has rescued his animals from slaughter and is a vegetarian); the place of the servant in the home (she is mad); the problematic role of the family (Dr. Selwyn is estranged from his wife); the place of the second home as an escape from the first (he now lives in this refuge); and the home as an expression of a desire to reclaim a prior condition (he longs for a past that is totally beyond reclamation of any sort). In what may be an allusion to the archetypal lost home in nineteenth-century fiction, David Copperfield's childhood house, the narrator notices deserted rooks' nests against the autumn sky. Seen from the perspective of history, a world of irony now haunts Aunt Betsey Trotwood's comic complaint against the optimism of her brother, David's father, who "takes the birds on trust, because he sees the nests!"[23] In Sebald's story, the one thing that cannot be taken on trust is the future.

The hermitage is located on the rundown estate of Prior's Gate in the county of Norfolk. When the narrator and his wife

Clara first arrive there, the "house gave the impression that no one was there."[24] All has fallen into disrepair—tennis court, greenhouse, and garden; the dilapidated greenhouse, of which we see a photo, is "on its last legs after years of neglect."[25] Charmed by the view from the window of the flat for rent in the main house, the narrator and his wife take up residence at Prior's Gate, and in the course of the story they come to know the interior of the house and Dr. Selwyn at the same time.

Prior's Gate is labyrinthine in its structure, full of "hidden passageways branch[ing] off, running behind walls" and doors that seem to appear suddenly: "Across the corridor, about a foot above the stone floor, there was a door in the wall. Through it, one entered a dark stairwell." The narrator imagines Prior's Gate in its prior state with "the shadows of the servants . . . perpetually flitting past. . . . behind the walls of the rooms." Although Mrs. Selwyn lives in the house, she is usually away, and the interior is inhabited by a seemingly mad servant named Elaine, who habitually "break[s] into strange, apparently unmotivated, whinnying laughter."[26] Echoes of Dickens's decaying Satis House and garden and Charlotte Brontë's gothic Thornfield, with its laughing madwoman, may be heard in these descriptions. Like Gateshead in *Jane Eyre,* Prior's Gate is a gothic dwelling despite its neoclassical architecture—a dwelling in which inexplicable rituals are enacted: "The logs were glowing in the dark. Dr Selwyn tugged a bell-pull to the right of the fireplace, and almost instantly, as if she had been waiting in the passage for the signal, Elaine pushed in a trolley with a slide projector on it."[27] At the end of the story a corpse is unearthed, and the narrator observes: "And so they are ever returning to us, the dead."[28] What stands out in the narration of these seemingly gothic details is the narrator's restraint, his almost dutiful lack of affect.

The palpable presence of unexpressed emotion is most powerfully evoked when the narrator views slides with Dr. Selwyn and his guest, Edwin Elliott, in the vast drawing room of Prior's Gate:

The low whirr of the projector began, and the dust in the room, normally invisible, glittered and danced in the beam of light by way of a prelude to the pictures themselves. Their journey to Crete had been made in the springtime. . . . I sense that, for both of them, this return to their past selves was an occasion for some emotion. But it may be that it merely seemed that way to me because neither Edwin nor Dr Selwyn was willing or able to make any remark concerning these pictures. . . . Whilst their images were on the screen, trembling lightly, there was almost total silence in the room. In the last of the pictures we saw the expanse of the Lasithi plateau outspread before us, taken from the heights of one of the northern passes. The shot must have been taken around midday, since the sun was shining into our line of vision. To the south, lofty Mount Spathi, two thousand metres high, towered above the plateau, like a mirage beyond the flood of light. The fields of potatoes and vegetable across the broad valley floor, the orchards and clumps of other trees, and the un-tilled land, were awash with green upon green, studded with the hundreds of white sails of wind pumps. We sat looking at this picture for a long time in silence . . . so long that the glass in the slide shattered and a dark crack fissured across the screen. That view of the Lasithi pla-teau, held so long it shattered, made a deep impression on me.[29]

Why do Edwin Elliott and Dr. Selwyn gaze at the image of the Lasithi plateau for so long? Are they remembering their trip of ten years ago or an earlier experience in Greece? The La-sithi province in Crete has been the theater of countless battles. Germany invaded Crete in the spring of 1941 and captured the island in ten days in an airborne invasion.[30] Do the white sails of the wind pumps remind the old men of that spring day in 1941 when German troops parachuted to the ground? Particles of dust provide an eerie but appropriate "prelude" to the image of a battleground. The "trembling" and shattering of the slide become metaphors for unstated emotion. We learn later that Dr. Selwyn had fought in World War I and that the Second World War was "a blinding, bad time for [him], about which [he] could not say a thing even if [he] wanted to."[31]

Instead of explaining the meaning of the image of the Lasithi plateau, the narrator tells us that "it later vanished from my mind almost completely,"[32] coming back to him only by means of another image when, a few years later, he is in a London cinema. All memories are lost, to reappear later only in the mutated form of traces—an idea that is reiterated when Dr. Selwyn tells the story of his life.

A Lithuanian Jew, Dr. Selwyn left his home at the age of seven with his family and emigrated to England. There he excelled in school, winning a scholarship to the Merchant Taylors' School and going on to distinguish himself at Cambridge. He changed his name from Seweryn to Selwyn and when he meets his future wife, the daughter of a wealthy factory owner from Biel in Switzerland, he tells her nothing of his past. They marry and live "in grand style" mainly on her money, buying expensive property and automobiles. Included in Dr. Selwyn's narrative of his life is this chilling aside: "The cars are all still in the garage, and they may be worth something by now. But I have never been able to bring myself to sell anything, except perhaps, at one point, my soul." Eventually Dr. Selwyn severs his ties "with what they call the real world"[33] and inhabits the hermitage, where he exists in a condition of homesickness, without any traces of his Lithuanian past except those in his mind.

The narrator and his wife are transient as well. They come from "mountainous parts," rent from Mrs. Selwyn, and then buy "a house one afternoon on the spur of the moment."[34] Early in the story Mrs. Selwyn delivers an amusing but "annihilating verdict on the way we lead our life" when she takes notice of their renovation of a bathroom at Prior's Gate: "Once the bathroom . . . had been painted white, she even came up to approve our handiwork. The unfamiliar look prompted her to make the cryptic comment that the bathroom, which had always reminded her of an old-fashioned hothouse, now reminded her of a freshly painted dovecote, an observation that has stuck in my mind to this day as an annihilating verdict on the way we lead our life, though I have never been able to make any change in it."[35]

In many contemporary works, human beings live in rooms that they do not own or inhabit for very long, and therefore rooms in which it is hard to leave traces of themselves. But from time to time they give to these rooms a little humanity, and, as long as this persists, interiors will be of interest to artists. In the scene in which his characters view the slide of the Lasithi plateau, Sebald seems to suggest that locating what is human about a given place—or identifying the memories in which feelings are so deeply buried—is a tenuous business. There is a sense in which Sebald pursues this business as a duty, very much in the spirit of Goethe's letter: "And so, even at an advanced age, we still have a duty to acknowledge the human— which never leaves us." In Sebald's case, to "acknowledge the human" is to recover and mourn it. Like the corpse that is unearthed at the end of the story, Sebald's interiors are not so very strange or "gothic" after all. They are merely human remains.

The eighteenth-century myth of Universal Man is now turned on its head. Whereas in *Robinson Crusoe* the image of Universal Man served to veil Bourgeois Man, in Sebald's story, the particular, historical qualities of Bourgeois Man are fully exposed, and the humbling universal fact of death awaits him: "And so they are ever returning to us, the dead."[36] The bourgeois impulse to reduce and reinvent the world in a confined space, imagining that this world is for him alone, for Man alone, has had far-reaching political and ecological consequences. Such an impulse was from the beginning closely connected to his claim to universal sovereignty. Yet in its domestic manifestations, this impulse has served more contradictory purposes. At the same time that it protects the experience of children, blesses the bourgeois with the memory of a sovereign space, and provides bourgeois men and women with an expressive mask, it also insulates the bourgeois individual from the world in ways that are blinding and debilitating. The artists who uncover these contradictions, in images of interiors that are at once charming, destructive, and vital, leave us with unanswerable questions about the modern experience of home.

Appendix

From Jane Austen's *Mansfield Park,* chapter 16:

[W]hat should she do? She fell asleep before she could answer the question, and found it quite as puzzling when she awoke the next morning. The little white attic, which had continued her sleeping room ever since her first entering the family, proving incompetent to suggest any reply, she had recourse, as soon as she was dressed, to another apartment, more spacious and more meet for walking about in, and thinking, and of which she now for some time had been almost equally mistress. It had been their school-room; so called till the Miss Bertrams would not allow it to be called so any longer, and inhabited as such to a later period. There Miss Lee had lived, and there they had read and written, and talked and laughed, till within the last three years, when she had quitted them.—The room had then become useless, and for some time was quite deserted, except by Fanny, when she visited her plants, or wanted one of the books, which she was still glad to keep there, from the deficiency of space and accommodation in her little chamber above;—but gradually, as her value for the comforts of it increased, she had added to her possessions, and spent more of her time there; and having nothing to oppose her, had so naturally and so artlessly worked herself into it, that it was now generally admitted to be her's. The East room, as it had been called, ever since Maria Bertram was sixteen, was now considered Fanny's. . . . She could go there after anything unpleasant below, and find immediate consolation in some pursuit, or some train of thought

at hand.—Her plants, her books—of which she had been a collector, from the first hour of her commanding a shilling—her
writing desk, and her works of charity and ingenuity, were all
within her reach;—or if indisposed for employment, if nothing
but musing would do, she could scarcely see an object in that
room which had not an interesting remembrance connected
with it.—Every thing was a friend, or bore her thoughts to a
friend; and though there had been sometimes much of suffering to her—though her motives had often been misunderstood,
her feelings disregarded, and her comprehension under-valued;
though she had known the pains of tyranny, of ridicule, and
neglect, yet almost every recurrence of either had led to something consolatory; her aunt Bertram had spoken for her, or Miss
Lee had been encouraging, or what was yet more frequent or
more dear—Edmund had been her champion or her friend—
he had supported her cause, or explained her meaning, he had
told her not to cry, or had given her some proof of affection
which made her tears delightful—and the whole was now so
blended together, so harmonized by distance, that every former
affliction had its charm. The room was most dear to her, and
she would not have changed its furniture for the handsomest in
the house, though what had been originally plain, had suffered
all the ill-usage of children—and its greatest elegancies and
ornaments were a faded footstool of Julia's work, too ill done
for the drawing-room, three transparencies, made in a rage for
transparencies, for the three lower panes of one window, where
Tintern Abbey held its station between a cave in Italy, and a
moonlight lake in Cumberland; a collection of family profiles,
thought unworthy of being anywhere else, over the mantelpiece, and by their side and pinned against the wall, a small
sketch of a ship sent four years ago from the Mediterranean by
William, with H.M.S. Antwerp at the bottom, in letters as tall
as the main-mast.

To this nest of comforts Fanny now walked down to try its
influence on an agitated, doubting spirit—to see if by looking
at Edmund's profile she could catch any of its counsel, or by

giving air to her geraniums she might inhale a breeze of mental strength herself. But she had more than fears of her own perseverance to remove; she had begun to feel undecided as to what she *ought to do;* and as she walked round the room her doubts were increasing. Was she *right* in refusing what was so warmly asked, so strongly wished for? What might be so essential to a scheme on which some of those to whom she owed the greatest complaisance, had set their hearts? Was it not ill nature—selfishness—and a fear of exposing herself? And would Edmund's judgment, would his persuasion of Sir Thomas's disapprobation of the whole, be enough to justify her in a determined denial in spite of all the rest? It would be so horrible to her to act, that she was inclined to suspect the truth and purity of her own scruples, and as she looked around her, the claims of her cousins to being obliged, were strengthened by the sight of present upon present that she had received from them. The table between the windows was covered with work-boxes and netting-boxes, which had been given her at different times, principally by Tom; and she grew bewildered as to the amount of the debt which all these kind remembrances produced. A tap at the door roused her in the midst of this attempt to find her way to her duty (172–74).

Notes

Preface

    1. Barthes, *Mythologies,* 138; 140–41.

    2. Rybczynski, *Home,* vii.

    3. Pocock, *Virtue,* 122; 71.

Introduction

    1. Benjamin, *Arcades,* 220–21.

    2. Benjamin writes of "man's imperious need to leave an imprint of his private existence on the rooms he inhabits" (*Arcades,* 14).

    3. Miller, *Speech Acts,* 190.

    4. James, *The Aspern Papers, The Spoils of Poynton,* 308.

    5. Sebald, *The Emigrants,* 21.

    6. On the first appearance of the word *bourgeois,* see Rybczynski, *Home,* 24. For a brief history of the term *middle class* and a discussion of some of the problems associated with defining it, see Eric Hobsbawm's "The Example of the English Middle Class." See also R. S. Neale's *Class in English History 1680–1850,* 1–46. In "The Bourgeois Interior," John Lukacs also discusses the difficulties associated with the word *bourgeois.*

    7. On the "bewitched element," see Bianconi, "Notes," 94. In "The Nautilus and the Drunken Boat," Roland Barthes' essay on Jules Verne in *Mythologies,* Barthes likens Verne's world to that of a Dutch painter, in which "the world is finite, the world is full of numerous and contiguous objects." Verne reveals his bourgeois lineage in the way "his work proclaims that nothing can escape man, that the world, even in its most distant part, is like an object in his hand, and that, all told, property is but a dialectical moment in the general enslavement of nature." In Barthes' critique, the bourgeois reduces the world "to a known and enclosed space, where man could . . . live in comfort: the

world can draw everything from itself; it needs, in order to exist, no one else but man" (65–66).

8. Westermann, *Art,* 56. See also the discussion of Jacob Ochtervelt's 1665 painting, *Street Musicians at the Door* (74–75).

9. Ibid., 47.

10. See Westermann, *Art,* 46–47; see also Willemijn Fock's "Semblance or Reality?"

11. Stewart, *On Longing,* ix.

12. See Frances Yates's *The Art of Memory.*

13. Westermann, *Art,* 69. See Westermann's brief disquisition on "the human interior" (69–74), which cites the important work of John Lukacs, Witold Rybczynski, and Simon Schama on this subject. Westermann discusses the emergence of the private study within the home and "the social and religious evolution of a reading culture" that is reflected in the many Dutch genre paintings that portray individuals reading. The cult of familiar letter-writing in the home, which arose in the eighteenth century, is also relevant to this development and to the emergence of the epistolary novel. (See the seminal chapter 4 of Ian Watt's *Rise of the Novel,* "Private Experience and the Novel" [174–207].) In a more recent literary-biographical study, Diana Fuss places emphasis on the *literal* space that makes the construction of subjectivity possible (*The Sense of an Interior,* 1–21). For a broader sociological and theoretical context in which to consider these questions, see Jürgen Habermas's influential *The Structural Transformation of the Public Sphere* and Michael McKeon's *The Secret History of Domesticity.* The latter elaborates on evolving relations between the public and private spheres in seventeenth- and eighteenth-century England.

14. Lukács, Georg, *Theory,* 41.

15. Ibid., 17; 122.

16. Quoted in Benjamin, *Arcades,* 218.

17. Lukács, *Theory,* 122.

18. See Liedtke, *Vermeer,* 138.

19. See R. S. Neale's *Class in English History,* 130–33. Neale calls into question the traditional three-class model as an adequate representation of the English class system as it changed and developed over the eighteenth and nineteenth centuries. He proposes instead a five-class model, one that takes account of the complex variety of the middle class. (To Neale, the middle classes include big property owners, military and professional men, the petit bourgeois, aspiring professionals, and other literates and artisans. He recognizes women as a subgroup in each class.) Broadly conceived, the eighteenth- and nineteenth-century bourgeoisie is made up of a group of classes between the very wealthy and the working class. As the following chapters in this work will

demonstrate, these middle classes were in the process of developing a powerful imagination of life in this period.

20. See John E. Crowley's *The Invention of Comfort* (141–70) for a discussion of the rise of the standard of living.

21. Benjamin, *Arcades,* 20.

22. See Benjamin, "On Some Motifs in Baudelaire," *Selected Writings* (henceforth *SW*) 4: 317–18. In "Evidence, Experience and Conjecture," Charles Rice draws on Freud's dream interpretation to understand the dynamics of both the domestic interior and detective fiction.

23. Benjamin, *Arcades,* 20.

24. James, "Honoré de Balzac," 468.

25. Rosner, *Modernism,* 12.

26. *Berlin Childhood around 1900* was composed in the early 1930s but not published until after Benjamin's lifetime.

27. See, for example, Didier Maleuve's *Museum Memories* (1999), Rosalyn Deutzsche's *Evictions* (1996), Kristen Ross's *Fast Cars, Clean Bodies* (1995), Keith Bresnahan's "Housing Complexes" (2003), and Paul Morrison's "Domestic Carceral in *Northanger Abbey*" (1991).

28. See also Thad Logan's comprehensive materialist study, *The Victorian Parlour* (2001), which details the department store–like contents of the Victorian middle-class home. Although the book does not focus directly on literature, the author attempts a "synthesis" that addresses the "inter-relationship of aesthetics and economics," analyzing the parlour as "an artifact that presents what Fredric Jameson called 'imaginary or formal solutions' to unresolvable social contradictions" (105–6). Both Rosner and Logan acknowledge the importance of the art historian Christopher Reed's collection of articles *Not at Home,* which appeared in 1996 (and which was followed by Reed's *Bloomsbury Rooms* in 2004).

29. Maleuve, *Museum,* 121.

30. Ibid., 150; Johnson, "Taste," 1.

31. In a discussion of "the social practice of decoration," Logan presents a number of theoretical perspectives (derived from Pierre Bourdieu, Michel de Certeau, and structural linguistics) to counter theories of decoration that "avoid questions of aesthetic value and experience," especially as these questions bear on the situation of women (*Victorian,* 76–79; 98–104).

32. Maleuve, *Museum,* 121; 151.

33. Eliot, *Middlemarch,* 431; 514.

34. Maleuve, *Museum,* 151.

35. Bhabha, "World," 446.

36. Ibid., 455.

37. Sebald, *Austerlitz,* 18–19.

38. Ellmann, *Oscar Wilde,* 309.

39. Shakespeare, *Lear* 2.4.263–66. References are to act, scene, and line.

40. Nietzsche, *Will,* 502.

41. Eliot, *Middlemarch,* 310.

42. Adorno, *Notes to Literature,* 172.

43. Adorno, *Kierkegaard,* 43.

1. Robinson Crusoe's Cave

1. See Woolf's "Robinson Crusoe": "[Defoe] comes in the end to make common actions dignified and common objects beautiful. To dig, to bake, to plant, to build—how serious these simple occupations are" (47).

2. In *The Secret History of Domesticity,* Michael McKeon compares Crusoe's "utopia of primitive accumulation" to that of "the domestic Housewife. . . . [The] propinquity of home and adventure is everywhere evident in *Robinson Crusoe,* and nowhere more than in the proliferation of 'my little Family' and of the 'household Stuff and Habitation' . . . that populate the scene of Robinson's greatest adventure, the island itself" (626).

3. Aristotle, *Politics,* 1220–23. Like Aristotle, Defoe (through Crusoe's father) emphasizes the safety of the life of the middle-class citizen: "middle-class citizens . . . pass through life safely," writes Aristotle (1221); "this way Men . . . in easy Circumstances slid[e] gently thro' the World," writes Defoe (5).

4. Defoe, *Robinson,* 4–5.

5. Ibid., 94.

6. Ibid., 5.

7. Crowley, *Invention,* 153–59. Crowley cites David Hume's 1752 essay "Of Luxury" and works by other Scottish moral philosophers, notably Francis Hutcheson and Adam Ferguson, as other examples of the trend to give "respectability to the new revisionist and relativistic view of luxury. . . . Their interpretations used the uncertainty implicit in traditional notions of luxury (as conditions in excess of what necessity required) to show that improved standards of living did not necessarily pose a liability to public virtue." In the work of Ferguson, "{l}uxury now referred neutrally to desirable possessions."

8. Defoe, *Robinson,* 94; 51; 110.

9. Ibid., 51.

10. Ibid., 117.

11. Sebald, *Austerlitz,* 16.

12. Defoe, *Robinson,* 117.

13. Ibid., 74–75.

14. Ibid., 81.

15. Ibid., 75.

16. In the late eighteenth century, the bourgeois desire for a second home or retreat often took the form of nostalgia for a rural cottage. See chapter 2, p. 56.

17. Defoe, *Robinson,* 133.

18. Watt, "*Robinson Crusoe* as a Myth," 298.

19. Defoe, *Robinson,* 139.

20. Ibid., 149.

21. Ibid., 220.

22. Ibid., 36 ("Firr"); 40–41 ("Hawk," "wild Cat").

23. Ibid., 54.

24. Ibid., 40.

25. Ibid., 124.

26. Ibid., 137.

27. Ibid., 71.

28. Ibid., 73.

29. Ibid., 81.

30. Ibid., 110–12.

31. The introduction of "primitive man" (or Friday) into this drama of human progress serves to further accentuate the achievement of rational civilization on the island. In *Virtue, Commerce, and History,* J. G. A. Pocock describes Defoe the political journalist as a leading defender of the new commercial order (176; 231), one who, like other writers sympathetic to commerce, was faced with the task of altering the negative perception of credit finance as a passion-driven form of speculation (99–100). To prove that speculative man was not a slave of passion, Pocock suggests, the "concept of barbarism" was injected into the debate, "that social or pre-social condition in which there was neither ownership nor exchange—or so it was thought" (115–16). Pocock does not discuss *Robinson Crusoe* in this context, which provides a more ambivalent commentary on the debate than we see in Defoe's journalism.

32. In *Mythologies,* Barthes writes of how "bourgeois norms are experienced as the evident laws of natural order" (140). The "flight from the name 'bourgeois'" (to which I allude in the preface) is neither illusory nor natural: "it is bourgeois ideology itself, the process through which the bourgeoisie transforms the reality of the world into an image of the world, History, and Nature. And this image has a remarkable feature: it is upside down. The status of the bourgeois is particular, historical: man as represented by it is universal, eternal" (141).

33. Defoe, *Robinson,* 94.

34. Coetzee, *Stranger,* 20.

35. Ibid., 21.

36. Defoe, *Robinson,* 23–24.

37. Sebald, *The Emigrants,* 1.

38. Defoe, *Robinson,* 9; 113.

39. Ibid., 142.

40. See Yates, *Art,* 369: "[T]he art of memory survives as a factor in the growth of scientific method."

41. Macaulay, "On Defoe," 273.

42. Dickens, "[The Want of Emotion in Defoe]," 274.

43. Benjamin, *Arcades,* 215–16; Defoe, *Robinson,* 110.

44. Benjamin, *Arcades,* 215.

2. Fanny's Room

1. Honan, *Jane Austen,* 24.

2. Austen-Leigh, "Memoir," 278.

3. Laslett, *World,* 5–8.

4. Honan, *Jane Austen,* 400.

5. Austen, *Persuasion,* 166.

6. Ibid., 152.

7. Stone, *Open,* 72.

8. Benjamin, *Arcades,* 20.

9. Austen, *Emma,* 353.

10. In "Sir Walter's Looking-Glass, Mary Musgrove's Sofa, and Anne Elliott's Chair," Laurie Kaplan emphasizes how Jane Austen "brings men and women into close proximity in the interior spaces" of *Persuasion.* "Austen establishes intimate, claustrophobic, and sensually charged spaces where characters are close enough to scrutinize each other and even to touch one another" (5). Kaplan further shows how objects of furniture are used to establish character—for example, the "sofa-bound Aunt Bertram" (2) in *Mansfield Park.* See also John Wiltshire's "*Mansfield Park, Emma, Persuasion.*" Wiltshire shows how the later novels "display a more intensified sense of the influence of place and environment on personality and action . . . and a much greater power of imagining . . . figures within the social and geographical spaces they inhabit" (58).

11. Austen, *Persuasion,* 119–20.

12. Austen, *Northanger Abbey,* 187.

13. Austen, *Pride and Prejudice,* 167.

14. The attitudes of both Sir Walter and Sir Thomas exemplify the theory of *embourgeoisement.* In Austen's world, many characters are to be found at the high end of the economic hierarchy, but all exist within the psychological parameters of the middle class.

15. Austen, *Mansfield Park*, 371.

16. Ibid., 366.

17. Ibid., 375.

18. Ibid., 421.

19. Ibid., 427–28.

20. Ibid., 384.

21. Kinkade, *Romantic*, illustration 18.

22. Austen, *Mansfield*, 250.

23. Logan, *Victorian*, 218–19.

24. Austen, *Mansfield*, 382.

25. Ibid., 418.

26. Perry, *Novel*, 230.

27. Ibid., 131. See also Susan Staves's *Married Women's Separate Property in England, 1660–1833.*

28. Austen, *Mansfield*, 379.

29. Ibid., 434.

3. Charles Dickens and the Victorian Addiction to Dwelling

1. J. G. A. Pocock writes: "No theory of human progress could be constructed which did not carry the negative implications that progress was at the same time decay, that culture entailed some loss of freedom and virtue, that what multiplied human capacities also fractured the unity of human personality" (*Virtue, Commerce, and History,* 147–48).

2. Cordery, "Public," 86. See also *The Spectacle of Intimacy* by Karen Chase and Michael Levenson for an illuminating reading of the intersection of private and public in Victorian England. The authors' general argument about "the thrusting outward of an inward turning, the eruption of family life into the light of unrelenting public discussion" (12) is especially striking when applied to public spectacles of personal life, such as the Caroline Norton trial. In their chapter on Dickens, the authors emphasize the uniformity of sentimentalized domestic spaces in Dickens more than the pressures of the street on the home and Dickens's different articulations of households and their contents as he developed as a novelist (my emphasis here).

3. Armstrong, *Dickens*, 12.

4. Dickens, *Dombey and Son*, 88–89.

5. Benjamin, *Arcades*, 220–21.

6. Fuss, *Sense*, 9.

7. See chapter 6 of Briggs's *Victorian Things* for popular Victorian ideas of "hearth and home" (185–228).

8. Chesterton, *Dickens*, 106.

9. Dickens, "Autobiographical Fragment," 771–72.

10. Dickens, *Pickwick Papers,* 90.

11. Ibid., 80.

12. Quoted in Schlicke, *Oxford,* 192.

13. Paroissien, *Selected,* 205.

14. Ibid., 200–204.

15. Ibid., 199.

16. Ibid., 193.

17. Ackroyd, *Dickens,* 608.

18. In *Victorian Things,* Asa Briggs discusses the emphasis on the "morals" of housekeeping in the popular literature of the day, an emphasis that he sees as peculiarly Victorian. At the heart of this morality is a belief in the civilizing influence of the home (190–91).

19. Paroissien, *Selected,* 200.

20. Dickens, *David Copperfield,* 167.

21. Ibid., 198–99.

22. Ibid., 232.

23. Dickens, *Great Expectations,* 82–83.

24. Ibid., 86.

25. Ibid., 261.

26. Ibid., 116.

27. Eiland, "Notes on Film," 151–52.

28. Benjamin, *SW* 2: 734.

29. Benjamin, *Arcades,* 222.

30. Dickens, *Great Expectations,* 87.

31. Dickens, *David Copperfield,* 247.

32. Benjamin, *Arcades,* 216.

33. For a long historical view and analysis of the movement of history toward credit, commerce, and the market, and the effect this had on human personality, see J. G. A. Pocock's *Virtue, Commerce, and History,* especially pp. 68–71 and 108–13.

34. Dickens, *Our Mutual Friend,* 136.

35. Ibid., 145.

36. Marx, *Capital,* 229–30.

37. See note 19 in the introduction regarding the work of the historian R. S. Neale.

38. Dickens, *Our Mutual Friend,* 50.

39. Ibid., 55.

40. Ibid., 73.

41. Ibid., 152.

42. Ibid., 730.

43. Ibid., 73–74.

44. Adorno, *Kierkegaard,* 44.

45. Dickens, *Our Mutual Friend,* 850; 886.

46. In *Victorian Things,* Asa Briggs shows the extent to which house dwellers were encouraged to become "clever buyers" in this period by popular writers on domestic subjects like Mrs. Beeton (190).

47. See the conclusion for a brief discussion of Benjamin's view of the preindustrial interior in *German Men and Women.* What Benjamin calls the "human" is relevant to Dickens's vision of the interior of an earlier era.

48. See Asa Briggs's *Victorian Things* for the rich historical background of the spread of commodities in Victorian England. In chapter 6, entitled "Hearth and Home," Briggs discusses the effect that the increase in the number of things in the home had on household management (see pp. 191–95). See also the art historian Peter Thornton's *Authentic Décor.* Thornton discusses the "dense massing of ornaments" that came into vogue in the 1860s (221). In literary and cultural studies relevant to the novel, recent attention to "things" may be found in works by Bill Brown, Elaine Freedgood, Thad Logan, and others. In *The Ideas in Things,* Freedgood analyzes "the fugitive meanings of apparently nonsymbolic objects" (4) in the mid-Victorian novel. Her chapter on *Great Expectations* focuses on the seemingly negligible references to "Negro head" tobacco in the novel and argues that "the repetitive mention of this tobacco . . . might be interpreted as a strange and circuitous attempt to memorialize a people who were very nearly destroyed by white settlement. *Great Expectations* 'remembers' Australian Aborigines . . . by way of this popular tobacco" (83).

49. Dickens, *Our Mutual Friend,* 112.

50. Dickens, *David Copperfield,* 170–71.

51. According to Logan, "interest in the 'foreign object' reached its peak in the last three decades of the century" although it can be dated back to the eighteenth century (*Victorian,* 182–83).

52. Benjamin, *Arcades,* 19.

53. Dickens, *Little Dorrit,* 236–37.

54. Marx, *Capital,* 229.

55. See Paul Jarvie's discussion of *Little Dorrit* in *Ready to Trample on All Human Law.* "In my view," writes Jarvie, "*Little Dorrit* is Dickens' most fully worked out 'statement' of the problem of financial capitalism" (6).

56. Benjamin, *Arcades,* 216.

57. Dickens, *Little Dorrit,* 236.

4. The Smell and Spell of "Things" in Henry James's *The Spoils of Poynton*

1. James, *Portrait of a Lady,* 172–73.

2. R. P. Blackmur, Leon Edel, and more recent Jamesians find in *The Spoils of Poynton* "a direct preparation for the great novels" (Blackmur, Introduction, 8).

Regarding the relative lack of critical attention to objects in the novel, my point here might be considered in the larger context of Jamesian criticism as Thomas J. Otten describes it in *A Superficial Reading of Henry James.* In his illuminating introduction, Otten discusses the "disciplinary mandate" by which the objects of everyday life "need to be brought forward *but not for too long*" (xix). Otten's chapter on *The Spoils of Poynton,* "The Properties of Touch," focuses on "the tactile relationships between persons and things" or what he calls "the touch of class" (40–41).

3. James, "Honoré de Balzac," 468.

4. Briggs, *Victorian,* 4–5.

5. James knew the work of Morris, whom he met on a trip to Europe in 1869. He also met Morris's great teacher, John Ruskin, and he consorted with Tennyson, Browning, and others in the 1870s and 1880s when he was living in London. As I have already suggested, in *The Spoils of Poynton* James is breaking with the realist tradition in fiction; as will be shown, he is also distancing himself from the intellectual legacy of the Victorian poets and nonfiction prose writers.

6. Quoted in Henderson, *William Morris,* 201–5.

7. Morris, "The Beauty of Life," in *Collected Works,* 76.

8. Carlyle, "Signs of the Times," in *Selected Writings,* 72; 75.

9. Morris influenced the Bloomsbury artists in their development of what Christopher Reed calls "domestic modernism." See Reed's chapter on the Omega Workshops in *Bloomsbury Rooms* (109–99). Reed writes of how "Bloomsbury's artists dedicated themselves, individually and collectively, to creating the conditions of domesticity outside mainstream definitions of home and family" (7). Their antibourgeois stance places them outside the particular emphasis of this book, but they represent an important development in, and are another indication of, the complexity of the interior design movement in the early twentieth century. See also Victoria Rosner's *Modernism and the Architecture of Private Life.*

10. James, *Art of the Novel,* 123. According to Asa Briggs, the "number of 'artistically appointed houses' was steadily increasing" in the late nineteenth century (188).

11. James, *Art of the Novel,* 123–29.

12. James, *The Aspern Papers, The Spoils of Poynton*, 129–30. Unless otherwise indicated, all subsequent quotations from the story will be taken from this edition, which is based on the original edition published in 1896.

13. Ibid., 149–50.

14. Ibid., 140.

15. Ibid., 142.

16. For a discussion of Freud's idea of fetishism in relation to James's story, see Sarris, "Fetishism," 61–64.

17. James, *The Spoils of Poynton, A London Life, The Chaperon*, (1908 edition), 78. The second sentence of the quotation is absent from the original edition.

18. James, *The Aspern Papers, The Spoils of Poynton*, 298.

19. The subject of fetishism in *The Spoils of Poynton* has been discussed in an article by Fotios Sarris, who gives a brief history of the treatment of the subject in James criticism. (He does not mention the relevant work of Nancy Bentley, which appeared at roughly the same time as his article.) Sarris offers a thoughtful interpretation of the story as it relates to both Marxist and Freudian concepts of the fetish, an interpretation that ultimately addresses vexed questions concerning James's stated intentions and his ideas of art. Sarris does not have that much to say about the more ancient form of fetishism alluded to in the story (which is of most interest to me here), noting only the "eerie rhetoric" and "curious" nature of passages in the story that attribute life to inanimate things (76). Rather than seeing Fleda as a character with special powers of seeing and feeling, he relates Fleda's character to what Pierre Bourdieu calls "political fetishism" (77). I am not as persuaded as Sarris that Fleda's fetishism (or even that of Mrs. Gereth) is to be understood in exclusively materialist terms. Nancy Bentley's *The Ethnography of Manners* argues that James's innovations in realist fiction are part of "a new way of seeing and writing about social life that developed in the later nineteenth century" in ethnographic writing as well as in fiction (1). "The literature of primitivism," she argues, "made the new commodity culture conceivable, capable of being imagined and written: it was the image of aberrant desire that writers saw in totemism that allowed them to describe an essential 'fetishism' behind civilized fashions and commodities" (117). Although Bentley's illuminating chapter on *The Spoils of Poynton* provides important background to the animism of objects in the story, it offers a materialist reading of this aspect of the story. Neither Sarris nor Bentley devotes attention to the interior of Ricks or to the suggestion of a fetishism that might go beyond commodity fetishism.

20. See Pietz, "Problem of Fetishism."

21. James, *The Aspern Papers, The Spoils of Poynton*, 178.

22. See Logan's discussion of souvenirs and foreign objects in *The Victorian Parlour* (96–98; 186–87; 197–201). Logan extends and revises the reading of souvenirs in Stewart's *On Longing*.

23. James, *The Aspern Papers, The Spoils of Poynton*, 134.

24. Ibid., 141.

25. The phrase "crude love of possession" can be found on ibid., 159. On alienation, see Sarris, who emphasizes the ways in which Mrs. Gereth "transgresses the limits of Marx's concept of the commodity" and seeks to preserve "the beauty of her own labour" ("Fetishism," 57–58).

26. Benjamin, *Arcades*, 205–7.

27. James, *The Aspern Papers, The Spoils of Poynton*, 141.

28. In *Meaning in Henry James*, Millicent Bell offers an alternative reading of the "spoils" that stresses their "disconnection from their origins, their loss of cultural meaning"; the "things of Poynton," she writes, "are truly 'spoils,' like treasures ripped from the temple or palaces of an enemy civilization by conquering barbarians." These "heterogenous bibelots of a modern collector, have, like the cultures they represent, lost any meaning beyond their individual aesthetic effect upon outsiders of another time and place" (209–10). I would argue, instead, that James lays stress on the aesthetic achievement of the collection. The fact that the objects are appreciated by "outsiders of another time and place" only makes them characteristic works of art, which, like Keats's urn, inevitably enter a cultural context different from the one that produced them. They may lose one meaning, but they gain another.

29. James, *The Aspern Papers, The Spoils of Poynton*, 281.

30. Ibid., 181.

31. James, *The Aspern Papers, The Spoils of Poynton*, 141. The phrase from "My Last Duchess" reads, "I choose / Never to stoop" (lines 42–43), Browning, *Poetical Works*, 368.

32. James, *The Aspern Papers, The Spoils of Poynton*, 308.

33. Ibid., 152.

34. Poe, "Philosophy of Furniture," 415–16.

35. Poe, "Philosophy of Composition," 480.

36. Poe, "Philosophy of Furniture," 415.

37. According to Diana Fuss, "In 1807 'interior decoration' made its official debut, designating a profession devoted exclusively to the growing interest in the artistic design of houses" (*Sense*, 16). Fuss cites the work of John Lukacs. See also Otten's *A Superficial Reading of Henry James*, which discusses interest in the aesthetics of interior design dur-

ing the period in which *The Spoils of Poynton* was published, drawing parallels between James's work and publications like *The Decoration of Houses* by Edith Wharton and Ogden Codman and "female magazines" (43–46).

38. Ruskin, "Traffic," 234. See also Briggs on the "morals" of housekeeping in the popular literature of the day (*Victorian Things,* 190–91).

39. Wilde, *Intentions,* 196; James, *The Aspern Papers, The Spoils of Poynton,* 142.

40. James, *The Aspern Papers, The Spoils of Poynton,* 161.

41. Arnold, "The Function of Criticism at the Present Time," 249.

42. Arnold, "The Study of Poetry," 306. In his autobiographical writings, James touches on youthful debates with himself over Arnold's faith in "culture" as "the most desirable thing in the world" (see *Autobiography,* 529).

43. James, *The Aspern Papers, The Spoils of Poynton,* 297–98.

44. Edel, *Henry James,* 460.

45. James, "Letters," 654.

46. Edel, *Henry James,* 519.

47. James, *The Aspern Papers, The Spoils of Poynton,* 164.

48. Ibid., 308–9.

49. Fuss, *Sense,* 164.

50. James, *The Aspern Papers, The Spoils of Poynton,* 320.

51. Browning, lines 97–98, *Poetical Works,* 675. Like the Duke of Ferrara, Andrea is another Browning fetishist of art, but one who rebukes himself here.

52. James, *The Aspern Papers, The Spoils of Poynton,* 318.

53. James, *The Golden Bowl,* 81.

54. As his critics have noted, this investigation is intimately tied up with James's development of a new language for expressing consciousness. See, for example, Sharon Cameron's *Thinking in Henry James.*

5. Virginia Woolf and the Passing of Victorian Domesticity

1. Rosner, *Modernism,* 12.

2. Woolf, *To the Lighthouse,* 32.

3. See Christopher Reed's *Bloomsbury Rooms* and Victoria Rosner's *Modernism and the Architecture of Private Life.*

4. Reed, *Bloomsbury,* 7.

5. See Benjamin, *Arcades,* 407.

6. Ibid., 20.

7. See Logan for a brief discussion of the revaluation of the idea of "home" in the nineteenth century (*Victorian,* 23–25).

8. Flanders, *Inside,* 4–5.

9. Patmore, *Angel,* 39.

10. See Woolf's "Ruskin." See also Deborah Epstein Nord's editor's introduction to Ruskin's *Sesame and the Lilies* for a discussion of the influence of "Of Queens' Gardens."

11. Elizabeth Langland points out that while Ruskin's argument is conservative, he "made familiar—naturalized—the association of women with notions of power and social regulation, however mystified, and so participated in the construction of a new woman" (*Nobody's Angels,* 79). In *To the Lighthouse,* Lily Briscoe, a type of new woman, achieves her vision as much through the power of Mrs. Ramsey's influence as through her own powers as an artist.

12. Woolf, *To the Lighthouse,* 207.

13. Woolf, *A Room of One's Own,* 91.

14. Victoria Rosner points out that Mrs. Ramsey's dictum to keep windows open and doors shut is derived from the hygienic regimen of Florence Nightingale. See Rosner, *Modernism,* 164.

15. Quoted by Martine Stemerick, "Virginia Woolf," 67.

16. Young, *Victorian,* 2–3.

17. See Quentin Bell, *Virginia Woolf,* 128. Woolf's sister, Vanessa, wrote to her that "it seemed to me in the first part of the book you have given a portrait of mother which is more like her to me than anything I could ever have conceived of as possible. It is almost painful to have her so raised from the dead. You have made one feel the extraordinary beauty of her character."

18. Woolf, *To the Lighthouse,* 262; 256.

19. Ibid., 291–92.

20. Ibid., 293.

21. Ibid., 309–10.

22. Woolf, "Professions for Women," 2215–16. The lecture was delivered before the Women's Service League.

23. Qtd. in Bell, *Virginia Woolf,* 134.

24. Woolf, *A Writer's Diary: Being Extracts from the Diary of Virginia Woolf,* 80.

25. Woolf, *To the Lighthouse,* 147.

26. Ibid., 218–19.

27. Ibid., 170–71. See Charles Rice's "Evidence, Experience and Conjecture" for an illuminating theoretical discussion of the relations between narrative and the domestic interior. The domestic interior

creates "the semblance of long experience through the techniques and practices of securing a private life" (291).

28. Woolf, *To the Lighthouse*, 168.

29. Ibid., 132

30. Ibid., 167–68.

31. Freud, "A Childhood Recollection from Goethe's *Dichtung und Wahrheit (Poetry and Truth)*," 112–13.

32. Woolf, *To the Lighthouse*, 146–47.

33. Woolf, "Robinson Crusoe," 45–49.

34. Woolf, *To the Lighthouse*, 158.

35. Ibid., 152; 155.

36. Ibid., 167.

37. See chapter 3, "1895–1897," of Bell's *Virginia Woolf*, 40–57.

38. Some of the most important changes in the status of women began in Julia Stephen's generation. The first women's college in England, Queens College, was set up in 1848; Girton and Newnham Colleges were founded in 1869 and 1871, respectively. The old professions—medicine, law, and theology—were very slow to admit women into their ranks, but teaching at the lower levels opened up in this period. Many fields of social service, such as nursing and hospital administration, were pioneered by women, often by individuals like Mrs. Ramsey, who began by doing philanthropic work. Woolf hints at the possibility of this sort of transition from private to public caregiver in her portrait of Mrs. Ramsey: "[Mrs. Ramsey] ruminated the other problem, of rich and poor, and the things she saw with her own eyes, weekly, daily, here or in London, when she visited this widow, or that struggling wife in person with a bag on her arm, and a note-book and pencil with which she wrote down in columns carefully ruled for the purpose wages and spendings, employment and unemployment, in the hope that thus she would cease to be a private woman, whose charity was half a sop to her own indignation, half a relief to her own curiosity, and become what with her untrained mind she greatly admired, an investigator, elucidating the social problem" (Woolf, *To the Lighthouse*, 17–18). For a striking analysis of the contradictions inherent in "angel in the house" ideology in Victorian middle-class culture, see Elizabeth Langland's *Nobody's Angels*.

39. Woolf, *To the Lighthouse*, 93.

40. Rosner, *Modernism*, 164–65.

41. Woolf, "Mr. Bennett and Mrs. Brown," 96.

42. Strachey, *Eminent Victorians*, 135.

43. Arnold, "Rugby Chapel," 11; 161; 182.

44. Woolf, *To the Lighthouse*, 280.

45. Forster, *Howards End,* 22.

46. Ibid., 155.

47. Ibid., 261.

48. Ibid., 297.

49. Rosner, *Modernism,* 163; 172.

50. Ibid., 5.

51. Forster, *Howards End,* 206.

52. Woolf, *To the Lighthouse,* 293.

53. Rosner, 4. See Rosner's illuminating chapter "Kitchen Table Modernism" in *Modernism and the Architecture of Private Life,* 1–20.

54. Woolf, *To the Lighthouse,* 38.

6. Bourgeois Memory and Dream in the Domestic Interiors of Ingmar Bergman

1. Mitry, *Aesthetics,* 349.

2. Bergman, *images,* 360.

3. Augustine, *Confessions,* 236–38.

4. Augustine also shows the influence of Plato, who had pointed to a knowledge that is latent in memories that seem to be based on the senses. Behind the sense-based memory is a deeper memory: knowledge of ideal forms, of realities our soul knew before it descended to the world of matter. Out of Plato's idealism came the memory systems of the Renaissance that claim memory's relation to a higher truth (see Yates, *Art,* 36). The vision that Isak Borg has of his parents by the lake at the end of *Wild Strawberries* suggests an ideal that goes deeper than sense.

5. See my discussion of memory at the conclusion of chapter 1. From its origins in English fiction in *Robinson Crusoe,* the bourgeois domestic interior is associated with memory.

6. Proust, *Swann's Way,* 7–9.

7. French and French, *Wild Strawberries,* 23.

8. Fuss, *Sense,* 151. Fuss writes: "Interiority, in Proust's view, operates like a surrealist stage set," producing a sense of disorientation in both the narrator and reader. "Proust draws specifically on the language and the technology of the modern stage" (206). As an experienced stage director, Bergman was also influenced by movable stage sets in the way he represents interiority in *Wild Strawberries.*

9. See Howard Eiland's translator's foreword, 5. My reading of *Wild Strawberries* here echoes his comments on Benjamin's treatment of memory in *Berlin Childhood.*

10. French and French, *Wild Strawberries,* 52–54.

11. Proust, "Bedrooms," 34.

12. Proust, *Swann's Way,* 13.

13. Benjamin, *SW* 2: 734.

14. Fuss, *Sense,* 197.

15. Wilde, *De Profundis,* 161.

16. Freud, "The Three Caskets," 522. In contrast to Isak's dreams of domestic interiors, which are associated with life, the opening nightmare of glaring walls and masks possesses a terrifying exteriority, in which resistance to the most frightening interior of all—the coffin—is the climactic event.

17. French and French, *Wild Strawberries,* 55.

18. Freud, *Letters,* 252.

19. Björkman, Manns, and Sima, *Bergman on Bergman,* 148.

20. French and French, *Wild Strawberries,* 29.

21. Wood, *Ingmar,* 73–74.

22. John 10:9 (King James Version).

23. Wilde, *De Profundis,* 137.

24. Bergman, *images,* 90.

25. Benjamin, *SW* 3: 369.

26. Bergman, *images,* 94.

27. Benjamin, *SW* 3: 375.

28. Bergman, *images,* 380.

29. Ibid., 366.

30. Bergman, *Fanny and Alexander,* 14.

31. Benjamin, *SW* 3: 375.

32. Eiland, translator's foreword, 5–6.

33. Benjamin, *SW* 3: 369.

34. For a striking discussion of the figure of the Jewish merchant in *The Golden Bowl,* see Susan Mizruchi's "Corporate America," 694–97.

35. Benjamin, *SW* 3: 369.

36. Sebald, *Austerlitz,* 24.

Conclusion

1. Benjamin, *SW* 3: 196.

2. Ibid., 167. The quotation is from a letter by Goethe.

3. Ibid., 170–71.

4. Ibid., 205.

5. Updike, *The Afterlife,* 10–11.

6. Sebald, *The Emigrants,* 5.

7. Updike, *The Afterlife,* 15.

8. Brooks, *Bobos in Paradise,* 11. Brooks describes the 1950s on pp. 18–25.

9. Updike, *Couples,* 331.

10. Updike, *The Afterlife,* 3–4.

11. Ibid., 15.

12. Dickens, *Pickwick Papers,* 621.

13. Updike, *The Afterlife,* 10; 17.

14. Ibid., 7–8.

15. Ibid., 15.

16. Ibid., 8–9.

17. Ibid., 13.

18. Ibid., 18–19.

19. Ibid., 226–27.

20. Sebald, *The Emigrants,* 10; 21.

21. Ibid., 7.

22. Ibid., 22.

23. Dickens, *David Copperfield,* 13.

24. Sebald, *The Emigrants,* 4.

25. Ibid., 7.

26. Ibid., 9–10.

27. Ibid., 15.

28. Ibid., 23.

29. Ibid., 15–17.

30. In accordance with a Greco-British agreement, a British expeditionary force of 58,000 landed in Greece in March of 1941. Germany attacked Greece in April of 1941, and by May 11, all mainland Greece and all the Greek Aegean islands except Crete were under German occupation. German airborne troops began to land in Crete on May 20, 1941, and fighting went on for less than two weeks before the Allied commander in chief was authorized to evacuate the island.

31. Sebald, *The Emigrants,* 21.

32. Ibid., 17.

33. Ibid., 21.

34. Ibid., 12; 18.

35. Ibid., 8–9.

36. Ibid., 23.

Works Cited

Adorno, Theodor W. *Kierkegaard: Construction of the Aesthetic.* Trans. Robert Hullot-Kentor. Minneapolis: University of Minnesota Press, 1989.

———. *Notes to Literature,* Vol. 2. Trans. Shierry Weber Nicholsen. New York: Columbia University Press, 1974.

Ackroyd, Peter. *Dickens.* London: Harper Collins, 1990.

Aristotle. *Politics.* In *The Basic Works of Aristotle,* 1127–1324. Ed. Richard McKeon. New York: Random House, 1966.

Armstrong, Frances. *Dickens and the Concept of Home.* New York: Boydell & Brewer, 1990.

Arnold, Matthew. "The Function of Criticism at the Present Time." In *Poetry and Criticism of Matthew Arnold,* ed. A. Dwight Culler, 237–58. Boston: Houghton Mifflin Company, 1961.

———. "Rugby Chapel." In *The Poems of Matthew Arnold,* ed. Kenneth Allott, 444–52. London: Longmans, Green, 1965.

———. "The Study of Poetry." In *Poetry and Criticism of Matthew Arnold,* ed. A. Dwight Culler, 306–27. Boston: Houghton Mifflin Company, 1961.

Augustine. *The Confessions of Saint Augustine.* Trans. John K. Ryan. New York: Doubleday, 1960.

Austen, Jane. *Emma.* Middlesex, England: Penguin Books, 1966.

———. *Mansfield Park.* Middlesex, England: Penguin Books, 1966.

———. *Northanger Abbey.* Middlesex, England: Penguin Books, 1972.

———. *Persuasion.* Middlesex, England: Penguin Books, 1995.

———. *Pride and Prejudice.* New York: W. W. Norton, 1966.

Austen-Leigh, J. E. "A Memoir of Jane Austen." In *Persuasion,* by Jane Austen, 271–392. New York: Penguin Books, 1995.

Bachelard, Gaston. *The Poetics of Space.* Trans. Maria Jolas. Boston: Beacon Press, 1994.

Bacon, Francis. *Essays, Advancement of Learning, New Atlantis, and Other Pieces.* Ed. Richard Foster Jones. New York: Odyssey Press, 1937.

Barthes, Roland. *Mythologies.* Trans. Annette Lavers. New York: Farrar, Strauss & Giroux, 1970.

Bell, Millicent. *Meaning in Henry James.* Cambridge, MA: Harvard University Press, 1991.

Bell, Quentin. *Virginia Woolf: A Biography.* 2 vols. New York: Harcourt Brace Jovanovich, 1972.

Benjamin, Walter. *The Arcades Project.* Trans. Howard Eiland and Kevin McLaughlin. Cambridge, MA: Harvard University Press, 1999.

———. *Berlin Childhood around 1900.* Trans. Howard Eiland. Cambridge, MA: Harvard University Press, 2006.

———. *Selected Writings,* Vol. 2. Trans. Rodney Livingstone and Others. Ed. Michael W. Jennings, Howard Eiland, and Gary Smith. Cambridge, MA: Harvard University Press, 1999.

———. *Selected Writings,* Vol. 3. Trans. Edmund Jephcott, Howard Eiland, and Others. Ed. Howard Eiland and Michael W. Jennings. Cambridge, MA: Harvard University Press, 2002.

———. *Selected Writings,* Vol. 4. Trans. Edmund Jephcott and Others. Ed. Howard Eiland and Michael W. Jennings. Cambridge, MA: Harvard University Press, 2003.

Bentley, Nancy. *The Ethnography of Manners: Hawthorne, James, Wharton.* Cambridge: Cambridge University Press, 1995.

Bergman, Ingmar. *Fanny and Alexander.* Trans. Alan Blair. New York: Pantheon Books, 1982.

———. *images: My Life in Film.* Trans. Marianne Ruuth. New York: Arcade Publishing, 1990.

———. *The Magic Lantern.* Trans. Joan Tate. New York: Viking, 1988.

Bhabha, Homi K. "The World and the Home." In *Dangerous Liaisons: Gender, Nation, and Postcolonial Perspectives,* edited by Anne McClintock, Aamir Mufti, and Ella Shohat, 445–55. Minneapolis: University of Minnesota Press, 1997.

Bianconi, Piero. "Notes and Catalogue." In *The Complete Paintings of Vermeer,* edited by Bianconi, 86–97. New York: Harry N. Abrams, 1967.

Björkman, Stig, with Torsten Manns and Jonas Sima. *Bergman on Bergman.* Trans. Paul Britten Austin. New York: Da Capo Press, 1993.

Blackmur, R. P. Introduction to *The Aspern Papers, The Spoils of Poynton,* 5–18. New York: Dell, 1959.

Bresnahan, Keith. "Housing Complexes: Neurasthenic Subjects and the Bourgeois Interior." *Space and Culture* 6.2 (May 2003): 169–77.

Briggs, Asa. *Victorian Things.* Gloucestershire, Great Britain: Sutton Publishing, 2003.

Brooks, David. *Bobos in Paradise.* New York: Simon and Schuster, 2000.

Brown, Bill. *A Sense of Things: The Object Matter of American Literature.* Chicago: University of Chicago Press, 2003.

Browning, Robert. *Poetical Works, 1833–1864.* Ed. Ian Jack. London: Oxford University Press, 1970.

Cameron, Sharon. *Thinking in Henry James.* Chicago: University of Chicago Press, 1989.

Carlyle, Thomas. *Selected Writings.* Ed. Alan Shelston. London: Penguin Books, 1971.

Chase, Karen, and Michael Levenson. *The Spectacle of Intimacy: A Public Life for the Victorian Family.* Princeton, NJ: Princeton University Press, 2000.

Chesterton, G. K. *Charles Dickens.* New York: Schocken Books, 1965.

Coetzee, J. M. *Stranger Shores.* New York: Viking, 2001.

Cordery, Gareth. "Public Houses: Spatial Instabilities in *Sketches by Boz* and *Oliver Twist* (Part Two)." *Dickens Quarterly* 20 (June 2003): 81–92.

Crowley, John E. *The Invention of Comfort: Sensibilities and Design in Early Modern Britain and Early America.* Baltimore: Johns Hopkins University Press, 2001.

Defoe, Daniel. *Robinson Crusoe.* New York: W. W. Norton, 1994.

Deutzsche, Rosalyn. *Evictions: Art and Spatial Politics.* Cambridge, MA: MIT Press, 1996.

Dickens, Charles. "Autobiographical Fragment." In *David Copperfield,* 766–72. New York: W. W. Norton, 1990.

———. *David Copperfield.* New York: W. W. Norton, 1990.

———. *Dombey and Son.* New York: Penguin Books, 1964.

———. *Great Expectations.* New York: W. W. Norton, 1999.

———. *Little Dorrit.* New York: Penguin Books, 1966.

———. *Oliver Twist.* New York: W. W. Norton, 1993.

———. *Our Mutual Friend.* New York: New American Library, 1964.

———. *Pickwick Papers.* New York: New American Library, 1980.

———. "[The Want of Emotion in Defoe]." In *Robinson Crusoe,* by Daniel Defoe, 274. New York: W. W. Norton, 1994.

Edel, Leon. *Henry James: A Life.* New York: Harper & Row, 1985.

Eiland, Howard. "Notes on Film." *Telos* 130 (Spring 2005): 141–64.

———. Translator's foreword to *Berlin Childhood around 1900,* by Walter Benjamin, vii–xvi. Cambridge, MA: Harvard University Press, 2006.

Eliot, George. *Middlemarch.* Boston: Houghton Mifflin, 1956.

Ellmann, Richard. *Oscar Wilde.* New York: Alfred A. Knopf, 1988.

Flanders, Judith. *Inside the Victorian Home: A Portrait of Domestic Life in Victorian England.* New York: W. W. Norton, 2003.

Fock, C. Willemijn. "Semblance or Reality? The Domestic Interior in Seventeenth-Century Dutch Genre Painting." In *Art and Home: Dutch Interiors in the Age of Rembrandt,* ed. Mariët Westermann, 83–102. Zwolle, Netherlands: Waanders Publishers, 2001.

Forster, E. M. *Howards End.* New York: Norton, 1998.

Freedgood, Elaine. *The Ideas in Things: Fugitive Meaning in the Victorian Novel.* Chicago: University of Chicago Press, 2006.

French, Philip, and Kersti French. *Wild Strawberries.* London: British Film Institute, 1995.

Freud, Sigmund. "A Childhood Recollection from Goethe's *Dichtung und Wahrheit (Poetry and Truth).*" In *On Creativity and the Unconscious,* 111–21. New York: Harper & Row, 1958.

———. *The Complete Letters of Sigmund Freud to Wilhelm Fliess.* Translated and edited by Jeffrey Moussaieff Masson. Cambridge, MA: Harvard University Press, Belknap Press, 1985.

———. "The Theme of the Three Caskets." In *The Freud Reader,* trans. James Strachey and ed. Peter Gay, 514–22. New York: W. W. Norton, 1989.

Fuss, Diana. *The Sense of an Interior: Four Writers and the Rooms that Shaped Them.* New York: Routledge, 2004.

Gay, Peter. *Education of the Senses,* Vol. 1. *The Bourgeois Experience: Victoria to Freud.* New York: Oxford University Press, 1984.

Gosse, Edmund. *Father and Son.* Boston: Houghton Mifflin, 1965.

Habermas, Jürgen. *The Structural Transformation of the Public Sphere: An Inquiry into a Category of Bourgeois Society.* Trans. Thomas Burger and Frederick Lawrence. Cambridge, MA: MIT Press, 1989.

Henderson, Philip. *William Morris: His Life, Work, and Friends.* New York: McGraw-Hill, 1967.

Hobsbawm, Eric. "The Example of the English Middle Class." In *Bourgeois Society in Nineteenth-Century Europe,* ed. Jurgen Kocka and Allen Mitchell, 127–50. Oxford: Berg Publishers, 1993.

Honan, Park. *Jane Austen: Her Life.* New York: Fawcett Columbine, 1987.

James, Henry. *The Art of the Novel.* New York: Charles Scribner's Sons, 1934.

———. *The Aspern Papers, The Spoils of Poynton.* New York: Dell, 1959.

———. *Autobiography.* Ed. F. W. Dupee. Princeton, NJ: Princeton University Press, 1983.

———. *The Golden Bowl.* New York: World Publishing, 1972.

———. "Honoré de Balzac." In *The Portable Henry James,* ed. Morton Zabel, 459–70. New York: Viking, 1951.

———. "Letters." In *The Portable Henry James,* ed. Morton Zabel, 627–81. New York: Viking, 1951.

―――――. *The Portrait of a Lady.* Boston: Houghton Mifflin, 1963.

―――――. *The Spoils of Poynton, A London Life, The Chaperon.* New York: Scribner's Sons, 1908.

―――――. *Washington Square.* New York: Penguin, 1984.

Jameson, Fredric. *The Political Unconscious.* Ithaca, NY: Cornell University Press, 1981.

Jarvie, Paul A. *Ready to Trample on All Human Law: Financial Capitalism in the Fiction of Charles Dickens.* New York: Routledge, 2005.

Johnson, Ellen Kennedy. "The Taste for Bringing the Outside In: Imperialism, Domesticity, and Landscape Wallpaper (1775–1825)." Paper presented at the annual meeting of the Modern Language Association, Chicago, IL, 2003.

Jonson, Ben. *The Complete Poems.* New Haven, CT: Yale University Press, 1982.

Joyce, James. *Ulysses.* New York: Random House, 1990.

Kaplan, Laurie. "Sir Walter Elliot's Looking-Glass, Mary Musgrove's Sofa, and Anne Elliott's Chair: Exteriority/Interiority, Intimacy/Society." *Persuasions* 25.1 (2004): 1–11. http://www.jasna.org/persuasions/on-line/vol25no1/Kaplan.html.

Kierkegaard, Søren. *Either/Or.* 2 vols. Trans. David F. Swenson and Lillian Marvin Swenson. New York: Anchor Books, 1959.

Kinkade, Thomas. *Romantic Hideaways.* Eugene, OR: Harvest House, 1997.

Langland, Elizabeth. *Nobody's Angels: Middle-Class Women and Domestic Ideology in Victorian Culture.* Ithaca, NY: Cornell University Press, 1995.

Laslett, Peter. *The World We Have Lost.* 3rd ed. New York: Charles Scribner's Sons, 1984.

Liedtke, Walter, with Michiel C. Plomp and Axel Rüger. *Vermeer and the Delft School.* New Haven, CT: Yale University Press, 2001.

Logan, Thad. *The Victorian Parlour: A Cultural Study.* Cambridge: Cambridge University Press, 2001.

Lukács, Georg. *The Theory of the Novel.* Trans. Anna Bostock. Cambridge, MA: MIT Press. 1996.

Lukacs, John. "The Bourgeois Interior." *American Scholar* 39.4 (1970): 616–30.

Macaulay, Thomas Babington. "On Defoe." In *Robinson Crusoe,* by Daniel Defoe, 273–74. New York: W. W. Norton, 1994.

Maleuve, Didier. *Museum Memories: History, Technology, Art.* Stanford, CA: Stanford University Press, 1999.

Marx, Karl. *Capital.* Vol. 1. Trans. Ben Fowkes. London: Penguin Books, 1990.

McKeon, Michael. *The Secret History of Domesticity: Public, Private, and the Division of Knowledge.* Baltimore: Johns Hopkins University Press, 2005.

Miller, J. Hillis. *Speech Acts in Literature.* Stanford, CA: Stanford University Press, 2001.

Mitry, Jean. *The Aesthetics and Psychology of the Cinema.* Trans. Christopher King. Bloomington: Indiana University Press, 1963.

Mizruchi, Susan. "Corporate America." In *Becoming Multicultural: Culture, Economy, and the Novel, 1860–1920,* Vol. 3 of *Cambridge Literary History of America,* ed. Sacvan Bercovitch, 666–709. Cambridge: Cambridge University Press, 2005.

Morris, William. *The Collected Works of William Morris in 24 Volumes,* ed. May Morris. Vol. 22. London: Longmans, 1910–15.

Morrison, Paul. "Domestic Carceral in *Northanger Abbey.*" *Texas Studies in Literature and Language* 33.2 (Spring 1991): 1–23.

Neale, R. S. *Class in English History, 1680–1850.* New Jersey: Barnes and Noble Books, 1981.

Nietzsche, Friedrich. *The Will to Power.* Trans. Walter Kaufmann and R. J. Hollingdale. Ed. Walter Kaufmann. New York: Vintage Books, 1967.

Orwell, George. "Charles Dickens." In *Great Expectations,* by Charles Dickens, 641–44. New York: W. W. Norton, 1999.

Otten, Thomas J. *A Superficial Reading of Henry James: Preoccupations with the Material World.* Columbus: Ohio State University Press, 2006.

Paroissen, David, ed. *Selected Letters of Charles Dickens.* Boston: Twayne Publishers, 1985.

Patmore, Coventry. *The Angel in the House.* Boston: Ticknor and Fields, 1856.

Perry, Ruth. *Novel Relations: The Transformation of Kinship in English Literature and Culture, 1748–1818.* Cambridge: Cambridge University Press, 2004.

Pietz, William. "The Problem of Fetishism, II: The Origin of the Fetish." *Res* 13 (Spring 1987): 23–45.

Pocock, J. G. A. *Virtue, Commerce, and History: Essays on Political Thought and History, Chiefly in the Eighteenth Century.* Cambridge: Cambridge University Press, 1985.

Poe, Edgar Allan. "The Philosophy of Composition." In *The Fall of the House of Usher and Other Writing,* 480–92. New York: Penguin, 1967.

———. "The Philosophy of Furniture." In *The Fall of the House of Usher and Other Writing,* 414–420. New York: Penguin, 1967.

Proust, Marcel. "Bedrooms." In *On Art and Literature, 1896–1919,* trans. Sylvia Townsend Warner, 33–38. New York: Carroll & Graf, 1954.

———. *Swann's Way.* Trans. C. K. Scott Moncrieff. New York: Modern Library, 1928.

Reed, Christopher. *Bloomsbury Rooms: Modernism, Subculture, and Domesticity.* New Haven, CT: Yale University Press, 2004.

———, ed. *Not at Home: The Suppression of Domesticity in Modern Art and Architecture.* London: Thames & Hudson, 1996.

Rice, Charles. "Evidence, Experience and Conjecture: Reading the Interior through Benjamin and Bloch." *Home Cultures* 2.3 (2005): 285–98.

Richardson, Samuel. *Pamela.* Middlesex, England: Penguin Books, 1985.

Rosner, Victoria. *Modernism and the Architecture of Private Life.* New York: Columbia University Press, 2005.

Ross, Kristen. *Fast Cars, Clean Bodies: Decolonization and the Reordering of French Culture.* Cambridge, MA: MIT Press, 1995.

Ruskin, John. "Of Queens' Gardens." In *Sesame and the Lilies,* ed. Deborah Epstein Nord, 68–93. New Haven, CT: Yale University Press, 2002.

———. *The Stones of Venice, Unto This Last, and Other Writings.* Ed. Clive Wilmer. London: Penguin Books, 1985.

———. "Traffic." In *Unto This Last and Other Writings,* ed. Clive Wilmer, 233–50. London: Penguin Books, 1985.

Rybczynski, Witold. *Home: A Short History of an Idea.* New York: Viking, 1986.

Sarris, Fotios. "Fetishism in *The Spoils of Poynton.*" *Nineteenth-Century Literature* 51.1 (June 1996): 53–83.

Schacter, Daniel L. *In Search of Memory.* New York: Basic Books, 1996.

Schama, Simon. *The Embarrassment of Riches: An Interpretation of Dutch Culture in the Golden Age.* New York: Alfred A. Knopf, 1987.

Schlicke, Paul, ed. *Oxford Reader's Companion to Dickens.* Oxford: Oxford University Press, 1999.

Sebald, W. G. *Austerlitz.* Trans. Anthea Bell. New York: Modern Library, 2001.

———. *The Emigrants.* Trans. Michael Hulse. New York: New Directions, 1997.

Shakespeare, William. *King Lear.* New York: New American Library, 1963.

Shaw, George Bernard. Introduction to *Great Expectations,* by Charles Dickens, 631–41. New York: W. W. Norton, 1999.

Staves, Susan. *Married Women's Separate Property in England, 1660–1833.* Cambridge, MA: Harvard University Press, 1990.

Stemerick, Martine. "Virginia Woolf and Julia Stephen: The Distaff Side of History." In *Virginia Woolf: Centennial Essays,* ed. Elaine K.

Ginsberg and Laura Moss Gottlieb, 51–80. Troy, New York: Whitson, 1983.

Stewart, Susan. *On Longing: Narratives of the Miniature, the Gigantic, the Souvenir, the Collection.* Durham, NC: Duke University Press, 1993.

Stone, Lawrence. *An Open Elite? England, 1540–1880.* Oxford: Clarendon Press, 1984.

Strachey, Lytton. *Eminent Victorians.* New York: Harcourt, Brace & World, 1948.

Susanka, Sarah. *The Not So Big House: A Blueprint for the Way We Really Live.* Newtown, Connecticut: Taunton Press, 2001.

Thornton, Peter. *Authentic Décor: The Domestic Interior, 1620–1920.* New York: Crescent Books, 1993.

Updike, John. *The Afterlife.* New York: Fawcett, 1994.

———. *Couples.* New York: Alfred A. Knopf, 1968.

Watt, Ian. *The Rise of the Novel: Studies in Defoe, Richardson, and Fielding.* Berkeley: University of California Press, 1957.

———. "*Robinson Crusoe* as a Myth." In *Robinson Crusoe,* by Daniel Defoe, 288–305. New York: W. W. Norton, 1994.

Westermann, Mariët. *Art and Home: Dutch Interiors in the Age of Rembrandt.* Zwolle, Netherlands: Waanders Publishers, 2001.

Wilde, Oscar. *De Profundis and Other Writings.* New York: Penguin Books, 1954.

———. *Intentions and The Soul of Man, The First Collected Edition of Oscar Wilde's Works.* Ed. Robert Ross. London: Methuen, 1908; rpt. Dawsons of Pall Mall, 1969.

Wiltshire, John. "*Mansfield Park, Emma, Persuasion.*" In *The Cambridge Companion to Jane Austen,* ed. Edward Copeland and Juliet McMaster, 58–75. Cambridge: Cambridge University Press, 1997.

Wood, Robin. *Ingmar Bergman.* New York: Praeger, 1969.

Woolf, Virginia. "Mr. Bennett and Mrs. Brown." In *The Captain's Death Bed and Other Essays,* 94–119. New York: Harcourt, Brace, Jovanovich, 1950.

———. "Professions for Women." In *The Norton Anthology of English Literature,* Vol. 2, 7th ed., ed. M. H. Abrams and Stephen Greenblatt, 2214–18. New York: W. W. Norton, 2000.

———. "Robinson Crusoe." In *The Second Common Reader,* 42–49. New York: Harcourt, Brace & World, 1932.

———. *A Room of One's Own.* New York: Harcourt, Brace & World, 1929.

———. "Ruskin." In *The Captain's Death Bed and Other Essays,* 48–52. New York: Harcourt Brace Jovanovich, 1950.

————. *To the Lighthouse.* New York: Harcourt, Brace & World, 1927.

————. *A Writer's Diary: Being Extracts from the Diary of Virginia Woolf.* Ed. Leonard Woolf. London: Hogarth Press, 1969.

Yates, Frances. *The Art of Memory.* Chicago: University of Chicago Press, and Routledge, Chapman & Hall, 1966.

Young, G. M. *Victorian England: Portrait of an Age.* New York: Oxford University Press, 1964.

Index

Page numbers in italics refer to illustrations.